JOHN CRIBBIN has spent most of his working career of 30 years as a writer, broadcast journalist, and is the author of the recently-released book *The Killing Times.*

He started out on the Melbourne *Sun* in 1950 and from there worked on newspapers in Australia, New Zealand and Britain. In 1969 he returned from Britain to join the ABC TV News Department. In 1973 he was appointed ABC Representative for New Zealand and the South Pacific. His assignments took him to Samoa, Tonga, the Cook Islands, Fiji and the rarely visited French nuclear testing site at Mururoa Atoll. On his return to Australia he produced and directed more than a hundred documentaries for the ABC's longest-running programme, 'Weekend Magazine'.

In 1978 John won the Walkley Award for a radio news report on the death of Sir Robert Menzies, and then again in 1981 for a television current affairs programme on a blind man, Eddie Ryan.

In addition to journalism John has written plays for radio and television. He is presently living in Melbourne, writing television drama and producing documentaries for private film houses, as well as working on another book. He has a wife and three children.

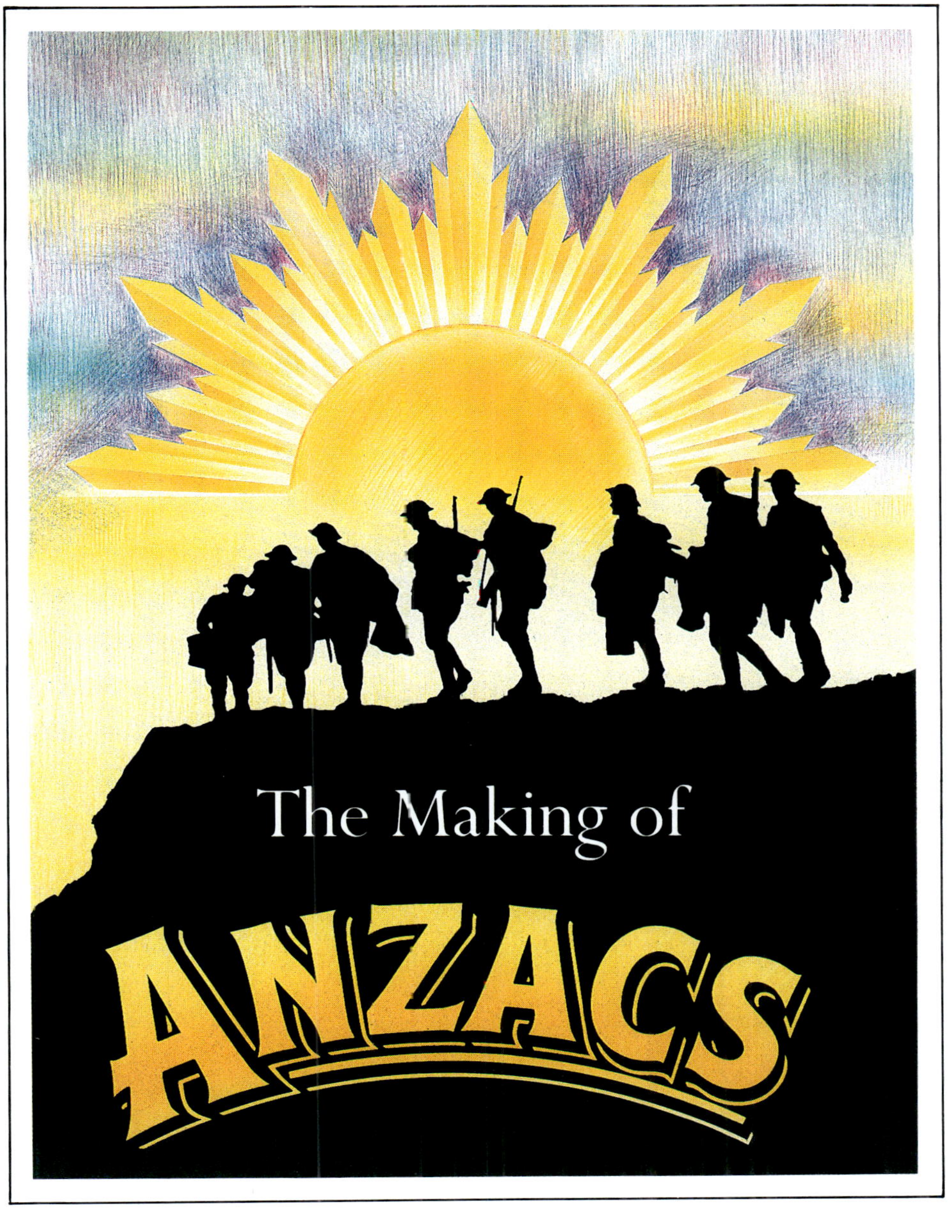

Compiled by John Cribbin

Stills photography by Greg Noakes

COLLINS/FONTANA

Also by John Cribbin
The Killing Times

ANZACS logo designed by David Lancashire
The maps on pages 12 and 13 were drawn by Anna Warren

The photographs on the following pages are reproduced, with permission, from the archives of the Australian War Memorial, Canberra (negative numbers in brackets): (A139) 3, (J1355) 7, (J355) 8 and 9, (E1847) 18, (G1126) 19, (C3193) 21, (A4497) 22, (E145) 27, (E16) 29, (Tasmanian Museum) 30, (E4852) 31, (portrait) 32, (E1073) 33, (E1220) 34 and 35, (E627) TOP 37, (E711) BOTTOM 37, (E594) TOP 38, (E3864) BOTTOM 39, (E4565) 40, (E3505) 42 and 43.

First published by Fontana (the paperback imprint of William Collins Pty Ltd), Sydney, 1985
Designed by Pam Brewster
Printed by Macarthur Press, Sydney

National Library of Australia
Cataloguing-in-Publication data:

Cribbin, John.
The making of ANZACS.
ISBN 0 00 636983 X.
1. The Anzacs (Television program). I. Title.
791·45'72

CONTENTS

'HEY, COBBER, DON'T FORGET ME!'

They were gipsy fellows with none but the gipsy law in their hearts, intolerant of restraint, with no respect for rank or caste unless it carried strength with it, difficult to handle behind the lines, quick-tempered, foul-mouthed and primitive men, but loveable, human, generous souls when their bayonets were not red with blood.

PHILLIP GIBBS, English writer and war correspondent, 1916

THAT WAS HOW MANY SAW THE Australian soldiers then. Those brave, tall, clear-eyed boys who proved themselves such willing and skilled participants in the game of war. It is not fashionable to eulogize soldierly virtues today. War and its trappings are passé, somehow soiled. 'Courage and heroism' and 'great feats of arms' are awkward terms, almost as unacceptable as 'hardship and self-sacrifice'. Yet fashions are ever changing. History shows that that constancy is war itself.

And what a war it was, that great conflict of 1914-18. For four years, most of Europe and its environs were shaken by a clash of arms of inconceivable scale and savagery. The *Encyclopaedia Britannica* lists casualties on all sides as 37 million. Thirty-seven million souls, dead or maimed, or reduced to madness, polluted by gas or disease, or blown into the oblivion of 'the missing'–their remains left to fertilize the fields of faraway lands.

It was a terrible war; a thunderous apocalypse, almost unique in the annals of the world for its profligacy of human life. A war of folly and jingoism, brutality and misery. The devil rode out and the world spurred his steed into a frenzy.

And yet it was a lovely war, too.

In Australia, there are still old men who look back on those times with wonder and wistfulness and a sentiment akin to love. Sometimes they talk of Gallipoli and Johnny the Turk, but more often they remember Fritz the Hun and places like Pozieres and Bullecourt, Villers-Bretonneaux and Passchendaele, Amiens and Mont St Quentin. Forgotten names now, most of them–places that in the main have reality only for those who were there. Yet this was where The Big Picture Show really took place; where the terrible ecstasy of war was most keenly experienced. In France and in Flanders, Armageddon seemed to be taking place. The Australian soldier was confronted with the profound revelations concerning death–its inevitability and its ordinariness. Those who survived were certainly changed, but also somehow broadened by the experience. As soldiers they discovered pride in themselves, and pride in Australian soldiery as an expression of a nation. Above all, it was where fellowship was sealed and comradeship extended into a sort of family bond, a brotherhood.

It's ironic that Australians and New Zealanders today equate the Great War with one phase of its course: Gallipoli. Yet Gallipoli, for all its valorous deeds and bloody exposition, was a sideshow, and in reality something of a shambles. It was a defeat bred of great hardship and suffering but yielding no tactical advantage. In many senses, the finest hour was the evacuation, for at least then the leaders had marshalled the imagination, ingenuity and good sense required to save life rather than squander it.

But at the Western Front there were no evacuations for the Australians, no retreats of any substance. They went forward most of the time, or confronted the enemy and stopped them in their tracks. They did extraordinary things in Flanders and France and proved themselves so good at war that Australian divisions – along with those of Canada and New Zealand – came to be used as 'shock troops', spearheading great battles that significantly changed the course of the conflict. The losses were terrible. On the Somme in 1916 and in the Third Battle of Ypres in 1917, Australian losses in each case exceeded in a matter of weeks all those sustained during the eight months at Gallipoli. When the war ended, Australian casualties amounted to 68 per cent – a far higher proportion than for any other force of the Empire. Sixty-eight out of every hundred men – almost a quarter of a million in all – dead, wounded or lost in the limbo of the 'missing'. And it was the Western Front that claimed most of them.

Such a loss . . . so far away . . . and for so seemingly slender a cause. Australia's population was only 5 million then, yet Australia committed so many to the mauling of that distant war. A tragedy. Yet a beautiful thing, too. These soldiers were brave; they had the innocence of idealism; there was a purpose in what they did; they believed in themselves so fiercely, they were never broken. And when it was all over, Australia had somehow grown up, and had the confidence to consider itself truly a nation.

ON 28 JUNE 1914, THE ARCHDUKE FRANCIS Ferdinand, heir to the throne of Austria-Hungary, was assassinated together with his wife at Sarajevo in Serbia, now Yugoslavia. Within six weeks, the great powers of Europe, including the dominions of the Empire, were at war.

In Melbourne, the left-wing newspaper *Labour Call* observed:

> It is unthinkable to believe that because an Archduke and his missus were slain by a fanatic, the whole of Europe should become a seething battlefield . . .

Unthinkable indeed – even for that coterie of continental nations that had strutted like a company of prima donnas for years. But for Australia, 16 000 kilometres removed from it all, it would seem now to make no sense at all.

Yet, then, it made all the sense in the world. Britain was at war. Britain was the hub of the Empire. And if Britain saw fit to take up arms over a dispute brought about by an 'Archduke and his missus', then Australia, her dominion, had no other place but at her side.

For almost a week before the British declaration, Australia was in a fever of war. Germany, Austria-Hungary, France and Russia were already marching, and the Turks were preparing to do the same. Yet the 'mother country' seemed to be standing back, uncertain of her duty in the face of an act that was generally considered to be 'a crime against civilization'.

In the first days of August, in the towns and cities of Australia, men and women gathered to sing the national anthem, to wave flags and declare their patriotism for the Empire. The country's leaders voiced the national sentiment.

Sir John Forest, the Commonwealth Treasurer, declaimed:

'If Britain goes to her Armageddon, we will go with her.'

The Liberal Prime Minister, Joseph Cook, stated:

'If the old country is at war, so are we.'

The Opposition leader, Andrew Fisher, soon

The recruitment sign goes up outside Victoria Barracks, Sydney, 1914.

to become Prime Minister, put it more ringingly still:

'Australia will stand beside the mother country to help and defend her to our last man and our last shilling.'

On 5 August, Australian time, the news finally came through: Britain was at war. So was the Empire. And with stout heart and almost universal approval, so was Australia.

Today it all seems so improbable. How could this little nation of 5 million people possibly commit itself to a quarrel that belonged to the other side of the world, a war brought to a head by the posturings of European powers impelled by nationalist purpose, territorial ambition, the advantages of trade and the rivalries of vain and incestuous monarchies? If the answer was, 'in defence of the mother country', we might ask today, 'Which mother country?' Would it be Britain or Italy or Greece or Holland or Yugoslavia, somewhere in the Middle East, or even Germany?

The 'mother country' no longer exists today; not in that form. There are many mothers, and they are more removed, as befits their relationship with children more independent and adult.

But in 1914, the umbilicus was strong.

In fact Australia *was* British. Ninety-six per cent of the population were of British stock. In the ten years before the outbreak of war, 400 000 immigrants had arrived from England, Ireland, Scotland and Wales. The way of life was largely modelled on Great Britain; much of the system of government was British, as were the institutional procedures, commercial practices, the religious background, the moral precepts and, of course, the language. Britain, quite simply, was 'home'.

Then there was the Empire. It was the grandest, most far-flung family of nations the world had ever seen. Those who were part of it, no matter what godforsaken corner of the earth they might inhabit, were said to be strengthened and elevated by it. From earliest years, the lofty concepts of imperial greatness were instilled in the Empire's children through tales of great derring-do. Citizens of the Empire had ventured to the four corners of the earth to enlighten uncivilized lands. They had tamed the jungles, pacified the heathen and brought order and fair play where anarchy had prevailed. The justice of the British Empire was untarnished, its sense of honour beyond reproach. It was righteous and strong and therefore unconquerable.

Many Australians believed that in the early part of this century. Some held to it with an almost religious fervour. Yet there were also those who were far less certain.

One of the things Australians had hardly begun to realize was the change that was already taking place in their character. Their blood carried the British strain, and the stamp of Empire was powerful. But they were also being moulded by the land they had settled. In the first place, they were bigger men than those of the motherland. The food was better, the air clearer, and settlement had involved them in physical effort that had strengthened the muscles and broadened the back. There was also a marked tradition of initiative and self-reliance. They or their forebears had shown a sense of adventure by crossing the world to make their mark in a largely empty, challenging continent. They were used to regarding each other as equals, paying little attention to the English system of class or even of wealth. There was also the peculiar alchemy brought about by the intermingling of English, Irish, Welsh and Scots – in Britain, manifestly separate; in Australia, a formidable blend. It took the war to prove that an Australian was not just a transplanted Briton; he was very much his own man.

The outbreak of hostilities had caught the Australian government – and the rest of the Empire – at half-mast. There was an election in progress. Prime Minister Cook and the Liberals had been blocked by Labor in the Senate, and the politicians had taken to the hustings. The familiar issues were the extension of federal powers and increases in pensions and the maternity allowance. War and even defence were subjects little considered. Even in late July, when most of the Continental powers had mobilized, Britain's and therefore Australia's involvement was hardly thought possible. Even when the coded cables warning of the Empire's impending commitment began arriving, the pressure of domestic politics overshadowed everything else.

Some of the messages from London were incorrectly decoded and vital information misunderstood. When the true situation did begin to emerge, the Prime Minister, Joseph Cook, did not even have the wit to call a Cabinet meeting.

Soon after, he was asked to state clearly the meaning and import of the intelligence the Government was receiving. 'I cannot talk about these things; they are too grave,' he responded. 'All I can say is that we are not asleep.'

Maybe not. It was difficult for the country to tell, and this was perhaps one of the reasons for the Cook Government's resounding defeat by the Labor Party under Andrew Fisher soon after.

One message that did get through, and with marked effect, was that Canada, with a population of 8 million, was offering Britain 30 000 troops. The unofficial report – quite wrong as it turned out – was published in Australian newspapers, causing the Cook administration further bewilderment. A contingency plan had been worked out with New Zealand that in the event of hostilities, Australia would send 12 000 men, and New Zealand, with a population of one million, would send 6000. Without checking the report of the Canadian offer, Cook announced that Australia would raise its contribution to 20 000 men.

It was a splendid gesture, full of patriotism and reflecting Australia's determination not be be outdone, at least proportionately, by its larger sister dominion. Canada had actually offered 20 000. Australia, with 3 million fewer people, had committed more men that it needed to demonstrate its loyalty.

Moreover, Australia did not have the men to send. There was a small permanent force and a militia of 45 000 who had undergone compulsory military training in the years before the declaration. But this was an army of boys, too young for war. A 'New Army' had to be raised from scratch. An army of volunteers.

There was what some called 'an atmosphere' about in those times, a sort of fever that related not to the duty of war, but the need for it. The conflict in Europe had sprung as if from nowhere, somehow owing less to the venalities of the Continental powers than to some grand passion that had erupted within mankind; a rage without reason or reference to right or wrong. Perhaps a juxtaposition of the stars or some primitive seasonal impulse had found the appointed time. War was suddenly glamorous and in vogue in Europe. In a matter of weeks, it had become so in Australia.

When the recruiting booths opened, the response was astonishing. Men came from everywhere: from the factories and shops, the schools and universities, the public service and the professions. In the bush, shearers and farmworkers abandoned the wool clip and the crops, joining pastoralists, drovers, kangaroo shooters, miners and railway workers, all linked in a frenzied rush to the colours. Brothers, sometimes entire families of them, turned out; fathers came with their sons; teachers and lecturers from the institutions joined their pupils; communities and factories gathered bands of men to step forward as a body.

The Governor-General, Sir Ronald Munro-Ferguson, cabled to the King:

'There is an indescribable enthusiasm throughout Australia in support of all that tends to provide for the security of the Empire in war.

The rush of recruits proved an embarrassment, not just to authorities but to many who had so enthusiastically volunteered. The Army accepted more than it needed but had to turn thousands away. It became a sort of selection parade for the First Eleven or the Premiership team. Men were rejected for minor imperfections of eyesight or age or height, or for having false teeth. Fronting the doctor, with braces down or stripped to the buff, became a test of manhood; a measure of virility and, by implication, courage. One man would be chosen while his mate was turned away. A father would find he could not join his son. One brother would be judged inferior to another.

There were men who left recruiting stations feeling demeaned. Faces were turned away. Some sat down and cried.

If rejection was a bitter thing for so many, it also ensured that only the best were accepted. This initial draft was the cream of the crop, the finest Australia had to offer. In the Dardanelles and later in France they were to stand out in manner and physique as men apart. This was something commented on again and again in writings about the Great War.

The British poet laureate John Masefield—referring to both the Australians and New Zealanders in 1916—was lyrical:

> They were the finest body of young men ever brought together in modern times. For physical beauty and nobility of bearing they surpassed any men I have ever seen . . .

They looked good. But would they make soldiers?

In fact, they were halfway there already. Approximately half of the recruits were country boys, brought up close to the bush, with the countryman's aptitudes and self-sufficiency. It was said that a bush lad had learnt half the art of a soldier by the time he was ten years old. He could build a shelter and sleep soundly in it, cook meat and bake damper, catch game, ride a horse and find his way across country by day or night. Most recruits – even those from the cities, which were then much smaller and therefore closer to the country – had at least some of these skills.

But they also had a characteristic that was perceived as a marked deficiency: they were not good at taking orders. It was not part of the Australian make-up to touch the forelock or to kowtow. The country boys in particular, rough and raw and imbued with the bushman's certainty that one man is every bit as good as another, hardly entertained the notion that anyone could command them to do anything. As the Australian war historian C. E. W. Bean put it, 'Most Australian soldiers had never in their lives known what it was to be given a direct order undisguised by "you might" or "would you mind" . . . They had never known any restraint that was not self-imposed.' But the tradition of the British Army, on which Australia's soldiery was based, was that if a soldier was given an order, he did it. At once! On the double! No argument, even if the command made no sense at all. If a British officer or an NCO had superior rank, he had God-given powers and an inherent superiority, not just as a leader, but as a man. The New Zealanders, and to a lesser extent the Canadians, with similar traditions of individuality and equality, had trouble grasping this concept, too. To the Australians, it was downright anathema.

When the initial training began, it became clear that the Australians were a disaster when it came to blindly obeying orders. Many of the old-style regular army officers tried it, and the result was confusion or outright defiance. Who was this feller telling them what to do? What right had he? What did he mean and what were the reasons for the orders he gave? It didn't take long for the officers to realize that if the Australian soldier was to be of any use at all, there had to be some compromise in the traditional British military approach. If an Australian soldier was to be told to do something, then it had to be explained. If an officer or NCO claimed superior knowledge or skills, then these advantages had to be clearly demonstrated. If he was to be accepted as a leader, it was no use relying on the stripe on the arm or the pip on the shoulder. A leader had to be seen as worthy of leading. Once that was accepted, he was followed with tolerable willingness.

It was hard on the officers, who had to rely on reason and example rather than insist on blind obedience. But they learnt, too. They became better leaders because of it.

When the first recruits marched off to war, they were half-trained and deficient in the spit and polish of British military tradition. They were slow to snap to attention, tardy with salutes, inclined to treat their officers as equals, not as masters. When the British caught sight of them, they judged the Australians an ill-disciplined lot, probably useless in war.

Worse, they were paid enormously well. At that time, the British Tommy received a shilling a day – although this was to be raised to three shillings by the end of the war. The New Zealanders got five shillings. When the Americans entered the war, even they did not match this, receiving the equivalent of four shillings and seven pence. The Australians from the outset received six shillings a day – five shillings outright and one shilling deferred. This bunch of 'lousy soldiers' were the best-paid troops in the war.

We are the Anzac Army,
The A.N.Z.A.C.
We cannot shoot, we don't salute,
What bloody good are we?
And when we get to Ber-lin
The Kaiser he will say:
'Hoch, Hoch! Mein Gott, what an odd lot
To get six bob a day!'

To the crowds that gathered in the streets of the cities to watch them march away, they were anything but an 'odd lot'. The mothers and

The going away . . . a jubilant yet poignant scene, Sydney, 1914.

fathers, the brothers and sisters, the wives and sweethearts cheered and waved and shed their tears. But the emotions were primarily of pride rather than apprehension. They looked so magnificent. Strong and tall and fresh-faced and sure of themselves. Initial training had been over a period of only six weeks. The serious business of soldiery was to be instilled in Britain under the eye of the *real* soldiers: those of the British Army. Yet the harried tutors in the Australian training camps had at least taught these raw, unruly colonials how to march. Left, right! Shoulders back! Head high! Rifles held in perfect alignment, the bayonets fixed so that they glistened in the clear spring light.

Their ages ranged from nineteen to thirty-eight. Most were around twenty-five – the apex of manhood in terms of physical strength, the time when immortality seems assured and the intimations of death are only a distant whisper.

Would they come back? Of course they would! Everybody *knew* that once the Army of the great British Empire got to grips with the enemy, the heart would be torn from the Hun and his miserable cronies. Everybody *said* the fight could not last more than a matter of months, perhaps only weeks. The might of Britain, France and Russia was already assembled to bring this about.

Poignantly, the first anxiety of many of the men who marched was not that they would die, or be maimed or become physically or emotionally broken. It was that the adventure might be denied, the thrill of the game bestowed on others; that the war would be over before they could get there!

The arrangements were that Australia's first contingent – 20 000 men, as promised at the outbreak of war – should travel by convoy through the Suez Canal and then to Britain to be

Tall, proud, ready for war. The first recruits, 'the cream of the crop', cross Princes Bridge, Melbourne, on the way to war.

prepared for action on the Western Front. It was a huge logistical operation. Ships had to be requisitioned by the Australian government, the vessels adapted to transport not only men, but horses, forage, stores, arms and medical equipment. There was the fear of German raiders, who had already taken a heavy toll of Allied ships in the Indian Ocean. The strongest possible contingent of protective naval vessels had to be marshalled.

Throughout September, troopships from most of the major Australian ports travelled the coast towards Albany, Western Australia. There were many delays. The German raiders were known to be active, and departure had to be timed for the moment of least risk. The New Zealanders also steamed in to join the convoy – ten of their ships caried 8000 troops. New Zealand, like Australia, had been carried away by the initial euphoria and lifted its contribution from the 6000 originally proposed.

There they were: Australia's and New Zealand's contribution to the Empire at war. Thirty thousand soldiers and sailors aboard thirty-eight troopships, every man waiting for a departure that seemingly would never come. Hurry up! Let's go! Time's running out, and it will soon be over!

Then, in the early hours of 1 November 1914, the convoy began to slowly move out from Albany, bound for Europe and the thunder of war.

It is doubtful that the Kaiser twitched in his sleep that night. Popular sentiment in Australia and New Zealand had him in a fever of apprehension. Not likely! The great clash of arms in Europe involved millions of men, many of them professionals, with huge numbers of trained men from the militia. What possible difference could a relative handful – a mere division and a half – of colonial civilians make to such a conflict? Moreover, this was a body of yokels, with only six weeks of training, who had hardly learnt to salute or take an order.

This scepticism was often expressed in the early days of the war, particularly in British military circles. There was a feeling that the Australians were so ill disciplined they would be unlikely to be trusted at the Western Front. Their only use would be in garrison duty in Egypt and India, thereby releasing skilled British troops more suited to fighting.

The troops aboard the convoy crossing the ocean from Australia and New Zealand were aware of this view. They discussed it often during the long days and nights of that voyage. They were insulted by it and rejected it utterly. They hadn't joined up for sentry duty. They'd enlisted for the 'real war' – the Western Front, where the challenge, the spectacle and the excitement could truly be found.

> Mademoiselle knows how to love, parlez-voo
> Mademoiselle knows how to love, parlez-voo
> She calls the diggers 'ma cherie'
> You get a good time in Gay Paree
> Inky-pinky parlez-voo.

Mademoiselle and so many would-be lovers were to be frustrated. As the convoy approached the Suez Canal, the Canadians, who were to share training with the Australians and New Zealanders, had arrived at their camp in the English county of Wiltshire and found conditions abominable. The place was knee-deep in mud and barely habitable. There was serious unrest.

In London, the Australian High Commissioner, Sir George Reid, who was well aware of the Australian soldier's character, contacted Lord Kitchener, Minister of State for War. Reid urged that, in order to prevent more serious trouble in England, an alternative training ground be found.

Kitchener agreed. The order went out to the convoy, and its destination changed. 'Gay Paree' was to remain far away. The Australians and the New Zealanders were to begin their overseas soldiering in Egypt, 'the land of sin, sorrow and syphilis'.

The arrival of 30 000 Australians and New Zealanders, coming in a single, unexpected deluge, in this ancient land, was an event that was to be long remembered. Suddenly Cairo and its environs had been invaded by another species: a race of giants. The Australians and New Zealanders were the tallest soldiers on any side in that war. This was the first time the world – and they themselves – were to realize it.

There they were, striding down the streets of Cairo, towering head and shoulders over the tiny, robed Arabs, who stared up at them in wonder. They stood out above the crowd like circus freaks. Not only could they be seen to be coming, they could also be heard, for they were as noisy and outspoken as country cousins who'd just come to town. A sort of band of early twentieth-century Midnight Cowboys ('Here comes Joe Buck, six-foot-one of eager, erotic muscle and rarin' for action . . .').

The British Tommies had trouble making any sense of them. They'd never seen soldiers of such size, nor with such outlandish disregard for the essential traditions of soldiering. The Tommy stood in awe of his officers, and in the teeming streets arms went like windmills in salute for each and every one. But the Australians almost uniformly refused to similarly recognize British officers of even the highest rank and, off-duty, paid scant regard to their own.

If the Australians were a surprise to the Tommies, so were the British to the Australians. Little men, so tiny, who thought differently and spoke in the strangest way:

'Ahr ya got a fag, choom?'

Of course they had a fag. The Australians were six-bob-a-day men, while the 'chooms' got only a shilling. Those who were paid like Rajahs could afford largesse towards their less fortunate brothers. They were friendly enough, the Aussies and the 'chooms'. But they were from different worlds. There wasn't that much they had in common.

The Australians and New Zealanders were dispersed in hastily improvised training camps around Cairo and for the next four months were drilled intensively in the art of war. It was hard, demanding toil, which rubbed the rough military edges off many, but not all. Boredom and restlessness were widespread. The more unruly element often got out of hand, and there were reports of brawling, drunkenness and thieving. The Australians at one time had such an unsavoury reputation that the better-behaved New Zealanders were warned to keep away from them.

Then, on Good Friday, 1915, the situation really erupted with the battle of 'The Wozzer'. It occurred in a street near Shepheard's Hotel called the Haret El Wasser. It was a red-light district, and an argument had grown into a riot. Houses were ransacked and the contents burnt in the street. Australians and New Zealanders were involved. The British military police were called, and shots were fired.

Order was restored only when they brought in 'the chooms' – soldiers of the Lancashire regiment. They were no longer the funny little men with the strange ways and odd accents. They were a disciplined force of the British Army, who came into the streets with cold eyes and bayonets fixed.

What was to be done with this unruly colonial bunch? What were they to be called?

The latter question had been decided in January 1915. Shepheard's Hotel was the headquarters of the Australian and New Zealand Army Corps. The administrative staff there had found the corps title too long and cumbersome for documents and telegrams. Something shorter was needed, and suggestions were called for from headquarters staff.

According to most accounts, it was Lieutenant A. T. White, an English Army Service Corps officer, who came up with the answer.

'How about Anzac?' he said.

And 'A.N.Z.A.C.' it was. Those who fought for the Corps became known as 'the Anzacs'.

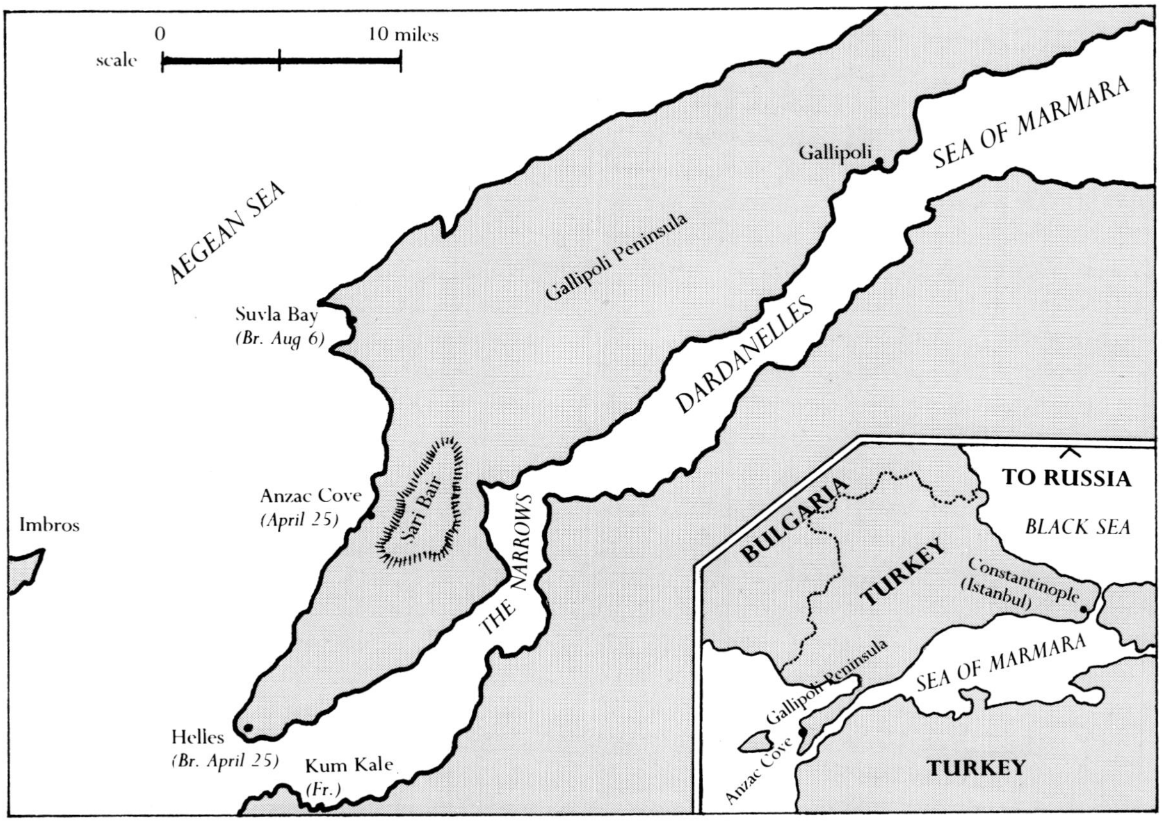

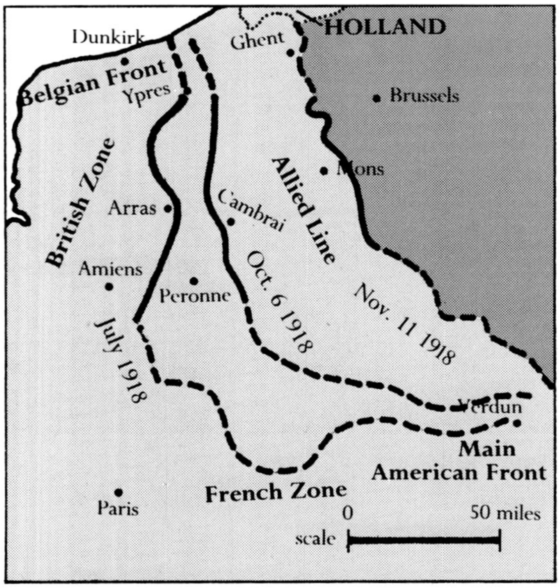

ABOVE: So near, yet so far. The stretch of mountainous land between Anzac Cove and The Narrows extends for only a few kilometres. Yet the Anzacs, during the eight months on Gallipoli, never attained the crucial heights of Sari Bair, overlooking the straits of the Dardanelles. Had the objective been achieved, the Allied forces could have paved the way for a naval attack on Constantinople, putting Turkey out of the war and opening the vital sea lanes to Russia.

LEFT: The breakthrough. The relatively dramatic change that took place in the front lines of the Western Front between July 1918, and the declaration of Armistice on 11 November 1918.

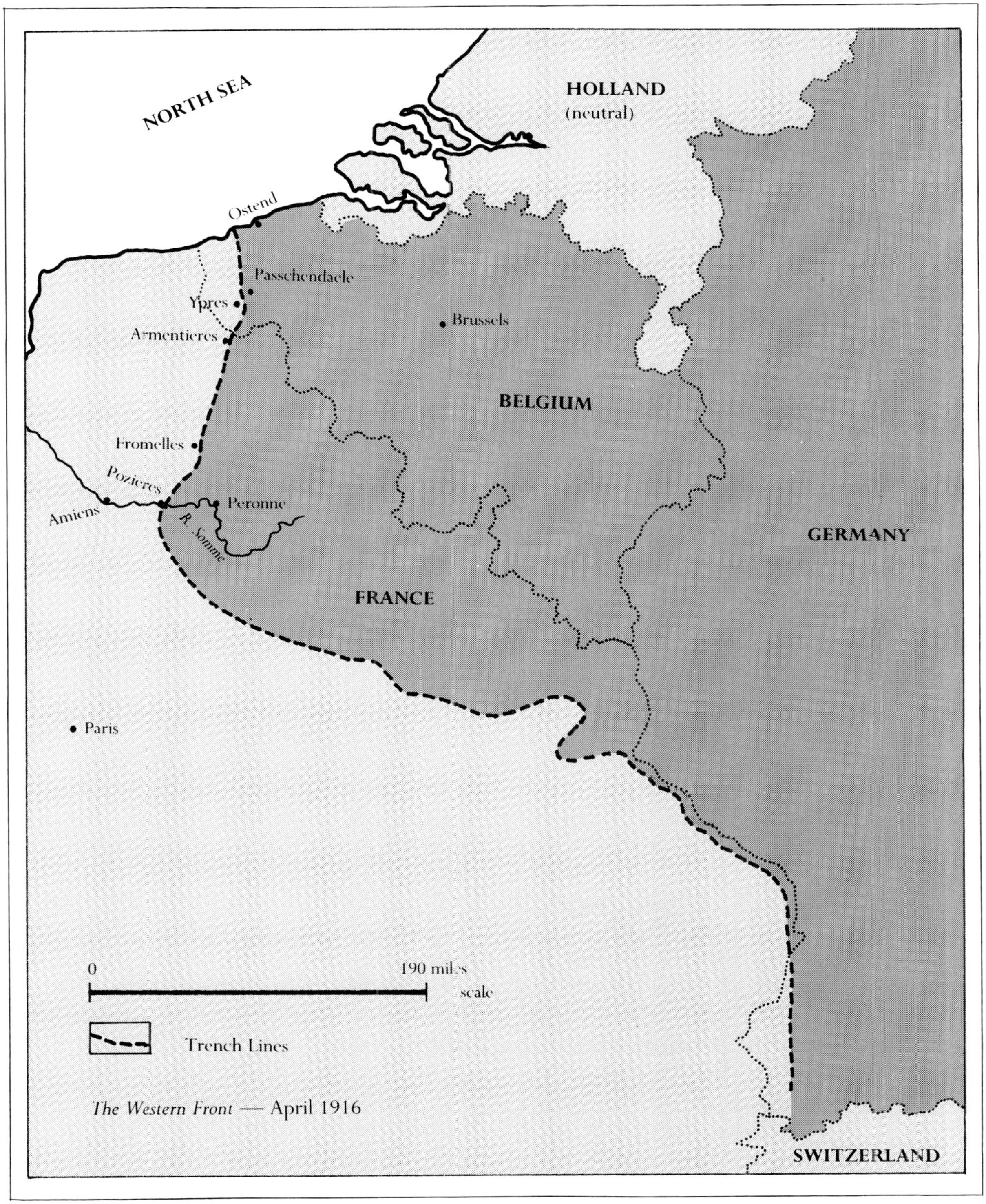

The Western Front — April 1916

This motley assembly of 'Joe Bucks' had a title that was to represent them to the outside world. Warts and all.

THE WAR IN EUROPE HAD NOT BEEN going well for the Entente of Britain, France and the other major ally, Russia. On the Western Front, the conflict that so many had assumed would last only a matter of months had become a battle of attrition. Trench warfare had begun. A line of opposing armies, millions of men, had dug in along a front extending across France and Belgium from the Swiss border to the North Sea. It was a new and dreadful form of war, governed by the murderous efficiency of the machine-gun and the might of heavy artillery. There was little or no movement. There was no opportunity for the traditional military tactics of outflanking the enemy, then sweeping past or encircling him. There *were* no flanks. Armies confronted each other eyeball to eyeball, committing thousands of lives every day in battles for territory often no larger than a cow paddock.

Yet there is no doubt that the Alliance of Germany and Austria-Hungary was doing better in this war than the Entente. The Germans' initial thrust had carried through much of Belgium and parts of France. The Alliance had also contained Russia in the east, reversing the Tsar's drive into East Prussia. Russia, theoretically a vast power with a population of 100 million and a huge army, was held at bay, further frustrated by Turkey's entry into the war on the side of the Alliance. The Turks controlled the Dardanelles, the narrow stretch of water between the Aegean and the Black Sea. Russia's vital southern gateway had effectively been cut off. Her ships could not voyage beyond Constantinople, and the arms and provisions she desperately needed could not get to her through the vital, Turkish-held straits.

It was Winston Churchill, then First Lord of the Admiralty, who pressed most strongly for a British assault on the Dardanelles.

Churchill had been greatly impressed with the big guns that the Germans had used during the initial phase of the war. The German howitzers, which had a high trajectory, enabled shells to be lobbed onto the heaviest fortifications with devastating effect. The big guns were the key to a breakthrough in the war, Churchill argued to the War Council. Yet the howitzers with their six- and eight-inch bore were relatively tiny compared with the twelve- and fourteen-inch guns of the capital ships of the British Navy. The First Lord proposed that the Navy be given the job of neutralizing the fortifications at the entrance to the Dardanelles, allowing its ships to travel through it, take Constantinople and clear the sea lane to Russia, which, re-armed and re-supplied, could then tackle the forces of the Alliance anew, relieving the pressure on the Western Front.

Theoretically, the plan was masterly. Yet in late February, when the great force of British and French naval vessels opened fire, a fatal flaw was revealed: the massive naval guns were not the equal of the smaller howitzer. The howitzer lobbed its missiles onto targets, whereas the naval guns hurled their big shells on a much flatter trajectory. The Turkish fortifications at the entrance to the strait were low-lying. The shells either missed them, ploughing harmlessly into the hillside, or only partly damaged the Turkish emplacements. Even after incredible bombardments, the Turks as often as not retained their ability to return fire. Some of the Turkish gun crews were driven out of their forts only to resume them later. Other forts failed to fire simply because they had run out of ammunition.

In early March, the first naval vessels entered the Narrows. Minesweepers had not completely cleared the waterway, which was no broader than a large river. Several British capital ships were sunk or damaged. The naval attack collapsed, and the fleet withdrew.

So began the tragedy of Gallipoli; as the war historian C. E. W. Bean puts it, 'through

Churchill's excess of imagination and a layman's ignorance of artillery'. Not only had the big guns of the Navy failed, their noise had woken the Turks to the danger of impending invasion. Gallipoli could have worked, and worked brilliantly, as a surprise attack combining naval and military forces. But there was no chance of a surprise attack now.

The Turks immediately increased their defensive forces from two divisions to six. They were heavily armed and well positioned to meet the land attack they knew would surely follow . . .

IN EGYPT, NEWS THAT THE AUSTRALIANS and New Zealanders were going to fight a war at last was greeted with enthusiasm, even joy. For four months they had been relentlessly trained in the Egyptian sands around Cairo, work that had immeasurably improved their soldiery – if not their discipline in the accepted British military tradition – but at the same time had left them utterly bored and frustrated. They'd joined up to fight the Hun. Instead they had been subjected to the seemingly useless tedium of 'slogging' beneath the African sun. The Dardanelles was not the Western Front. But at least it was an alternative to Egypt, a place they were sick to death of. The Dardanelles would do.

At the outset, the Australian officers had warned that the task would not be easy. 'Some of you may die,' they had said. But what did that mean? How could the image of death mean anything to those who had never been touched by war? They were young and at the peak of their physical strength and assured of their own immortality. Death was an abstract; a matter that concerned others, hardly conceivable as a personal thing.

The plan was to land 80 000 men at selected points along the western and southern reaches of the peninsula. The force was to be made up of five divisions: one French, two British and two of Australians and New Zealanders. The French were to stage a largely diversionary attack at Kum Kale on the eastern peninsula, the British a major assault on the Gallipoli or western peninsula at Helles, and the Australians and New Zealanders at a third point twenty-four kilometres further north at Gaba Tepe, where there was a half-moon beach that was to become known as Anzac Cove.

The strategy was to engage and neutralize the Turkish defenders, take the heights overlooking the straits and pave the way for the conquest of the Dardanelles.

The invading force was concentrating on a relatively small patch of Turkish soil. In places it was only eight kilometres wide from the landing beach to the straits. The objective seemed puny in the face of such a force, supported as it was by the British Navy, briefed to provide massive covering fire. There was a certain arrogance amongst the planners of this operation, who saw the Turks as opponents who would crumple or turn and run from the Empire's might.

The Turks were underestimated. Their defending force had been increased to 62 000, cleverly positioned and largely dug in along the beaches and on the heights. They were not going anywhere. They were ready and waiting.

The conditions were perfect for a landing. In the early hours of the morning of Sunday, 25 April 1915, the Anzac divisions approached their objective at Gaba Tepe. The sea was smooth, the moon down. The men who only a few months before had so eagerly sought the opportunity of war were now to experience it.

In the darkeness before dawn, they slithered down ropes from the ships into longboats that were to take them to the beach. There were between thirty and forty men in each boat. Each soldier was kitted with two days' rations, 200 rounds of ammunition, trenching tools and two empty sandbags. The longboats were towed by the warships to the vicinity of the beach, then rowed towards shore. The sea was a mass of ships, but they were hidden by the darkness. The only sound was the soft swish of oars propelling men towards the cliffs outlined against the night sky.

For a moment, it seemed as though the Turks were asleep or absent altogether—there was neither sight nor sound of life. The men were crouched low in the boats, their hearts pounding but their hopes lifting. Success! A complete surprise.

Then there was a flash of yellow light, and shouts were heard from the high ground above the beach. A rifle fired, more shots followed. Suddenly bullets were spitting onto the beach. Even before the first boatloads reached the shore, the Turkish fire was striking sparks from the shingles along the water's edge. Some men were hit before they could leave their boats. Others jumped into deep water, to be dragged down by their heavy kit, some drowning. The majority were wading through the shallows, and then the beach was seething with men, running for their lives towards the shelter of the cliffs. Many were falling.

Lieutenant E. W. Talbot Smith, aged twenty-two, a Duntroon graduate from Adelaide, was first ashore from his boat.

'Come on boys,' he shouted. 'They can't hit you!'

Within a week he was dead from wounds received on that day.

Some boats were landed in the wrong place. Those of the Australian Third Infantry Brigade beached on the far side of Anzac Cove, more than one and a half kilometres from their scheduled destination. As the troops ran for available cover, the officers stared in confusion at terrain utterly different from what they had been briefed to expect.

But the order had been dinned into every officer and every man:

'Whatever the opposition, you must go forward!'

And forward they went—up the cliffs and mounds and into the valleys. Within a matter of minutes, a rough line of about six companies was hacking a way through the thick gorse that covered most of the hillsides. The growth was so dense, it posed an exhausting obstacle. Clutching the tree-like roots, the men hauled themselves upwards. In the dawn light, sailors aboard the ships moored offshore cheered as the troops were seen flinging themselves like cats at the precipitous slopes of the plateau.

As the first assault progressed, more and more boats moved towards the beach, followed by larger vessels bearing stores and ammunition. There were many losses during those initial hours, but the landing had been achieved and the foothold gained. Now it was time to assault and gain the Turkish-held heights.

The names of these objectives were to occur again and again in the terrible Gallipoli campaign: Walker's Ridge, Russell's Top, Lone Pine, The Nek, Battleship Hill, Baby 700. Many of these were reached and taken in that first assault. Yet, because of the height and difficulty of the terrain, the furthest extent of the advance was not much more than one and a half kilometres from the beachfront.

Then, at 10.30 a.m., the Turks launched the first of two counterattacks. Reinforcements had been quickly marshalled, machines and heavy artillery positioned. Down the hillside came the Turks in their thousands.

'Allah! Mohammed!'

Throughout that first day, the lower hills around Anzac Cove were filled with the sounds of war. In the gullies and the open scrub lands and at the approaches to the peaks, a sea of men were involved in combat, and the ground was thick with dead and wounded. There was a ceaseless storm of rifle and machine-gun fire, and shrapnel from the Turkish artillery on the furthest heights cut a swathe through the troops still desperately scrabbling up the almost sheer slopes towards Turkish entrenchments. There was little or no cover other than the lee of a hill or the gorse, which offered a miserable, inhospitable hiding place.

Even the protective fire of the Navy's great ships moored offshore was denied. The fighting was so dispersed and confused that the naval officers were eventually forced to hold fire altogether, because they could not tell who was friend and who was foe, nor where the advance positions were.

Thirteen thousand troops had been landed on the first day. Almost 3000 were casualties, and the hillsides harboured the bodies of many more. Even at that early stage, Gallipoli was perceived as a disaster. The initial force was too small, the terrain too devastatingly difficult and the Turks too numerous and well prepared.

That night, the commander of the ANZAC Corps, Lieutenant General Birdwood, on the advice of his senior officers, sent a letter to General Sir Ian Hamilton, Commander of the Dardanelles Forces, urging evacuation.

General Hamilton, sleeping aboard the flagship *Queen Elizabeth*, had been woken by a senior aide calling,

'Sir Ian – a question of life and death – you must settle it!'

Hamilton, still in pyjamas, consulted with his staff officers, then wrote the reply:

'You have got through the difficult business, now you only have to dig, dig, dig, until you are safe.'

And that's what they did. Throughout the night and for many days after, the Anzacs burrowed into the hillsides around Gaba Tepe, to sustain a mission that was virtually hopeless, and to support the reputations of those who had planned it and failed.

What did they make of it all, those young men who only a few months before had so eagerly besieged the recruiting offices in Australian towns and cities, almost begging for the privilege of fighting?

They had been selected as the best, while so many had been rejected. Men had cried because they could not take part in the game. Yet within hours and sometimes even minutes at Gallipoli, they'd seen their fellows cut down and their own lives hanging as if by a thread.

'Joe Buck' had come to the big city looking for a dream and found a ghetto that could devour him.

Despite the murderous experience of the landing, the Anzacs had not been cowed by their first taste of battle. Birdwood's recommendation for withdrawal had been put forward in the belief that the troops had come close to being demoralized on that first day. But Birdwood's view had been based on the degree of exhaustion shown by fighting men on return to the beach, and the flow of dead and wounded. In the forward lines, the troops in general were anything but demoralized. They had been blooded in battle, but they were hanging on with great determination. Most of these soliders were not aware that evacuation had been contemplated, let alone proposed.

They had been underrated. Even on the first day, they had put down fears that they would be too undisciplined to fight. Their soldiery had been raw but impressive. They'd gone forward or hung on under impossible conditions, and they had followed orders decisively.

In the next eight months the Anzacs were to consolidate their reputation as exceptional soldiers. Dug in along those wretched hillsides, engaged in endless attack and counterattack, until the hills and valleys were smothered with dead, they withstood the rigours of battle and the scourge of disease. Within the first few weeks, fly-borne sickness had affected most of them. Not only did they have to withstand the strain of fighting day and night, they were cursed by illnesses that sapped their strength.

The tall, fit men who had appeared so striking in the streets of Cairo were reduced to gaunt shadows. Almost every man had been afflicted with dysentery, enteric fever or paratyphoid. At

The trench was the miserable refuge that symbolized the towering experience of war.

one stage, almost 200 sick a day were being shipped from Anzac to hospitals in Lemnos and Egypt. The wastage through sickness was so great that medical authorities adopted a policy of encouraging men to continue their regimental duties as long as they had an ounce of strength to 'carry on'.

And here is the paradox: so many were willing, even eager, to do so. Not only the sick but those with lesser wounds often refused to leave the trenches, opting to stay with their mates rather than be shipped out for treatment and rest. It was a sort of code of honour, a reinforcement of the ethic of 'mateship' that had its beginning in the traditions of the Australian bush and had been strengthened in Egypt. Now it had crystallized and taken a powerful form, almost impossible to comprehend from the distant and so different perspectives of today.

Inside a captured Turkish trench at Lone Pine, August 1915.

C. E. W. Bean comes closest to expressing the tenor of what it was all about then:

> To be the sort of man who would give way when his mates were trusting in his firmness; to be the sort of man who would fail when the line required his endurance; to live the rest of his life haunted by the knowledge that he had set his hand to a soldier's task and had lacked the grit to carry it through – that was the prospect that these men could not face.
>
> Life was very dear, but life was not worth living unless they could be true to their idea of Australian manhood.

They *were* true. They held on, clinging to the miserable toeholds they had gained in the initial attacks and hardly advanced over many months.

In August came the last chance: the final desperate attempt to break out and gain the upper heights. Reinforcements had been brought in progressively – although not enough to replace adequately the numbers lost through battle and sickness. At Suvla Bay, the British landed divisions that were briefed to attack from the opposite side of the tallest peak, Sari Bair, link with the Anzacs and break the deadlock once and for all.

There were scenes of great poignancy as this attack was launched. It was to be the most difficult and deadly of all. The peaks towered above. Many of the slopes were almost vertical. Waiting were the machine-guns of the Turks.

Death was afoot just above the rim of every Anzac trench.

A party of men from the Fourth Brigade gathered, waiting for the call to attack. It was night, and a Turkish star shell blazed in the dark sky. The men began to sing 'Lead Kindly Light'.

> Lead kindly light, amid the encircling gloom.
> Lead Thou me on.
> The night is dark and I am far from home;
> Lead Thou me on.
> Keep Thou my feet; I do not ask to see
> The distant scene – one step enough for me . . .

Then, over they went! For four days, some of the most ferocious fighting of the Gallipoli campaign took place at Hill 60, The Nek, Chunuk Bair and Lone Pine, and astonishing feats of soldiery were performed. The casualties numbered thousands.

But, as so often was the case with Gallipoli, there was a blunder, and it was all in vain. While the Anzacs were fighting on the high slopes, the British had landed at Suvla on the opposite side of the mountain but had not been commanded to attack. For twelve hours they sat on the beach. When their commander – a general aptly named Stopford – finally heeded the frenzied messages to send his troops forward, it was too late. The Turks were ready. The opportunity had been lost.

The British historian B. H. Liddell Hart refers to Gallipoli as a campaign 'marred by a chain of errors almost unrivalled, even in British history'.

There were almost 140 000 casualties: 7500 New Zealanders, 27 000 French and 85 000 of the British Army and Navy. Australian casualties were 26 000 – less than a third of the British, and fewer even than the French.

Contrary to common belief in Australasia, it was not even a campaign conducted primarily by Australians and New Zealanders, but a tragedy shared at much greater cost.

But on those two nights of December 1915, as the 40 000 Anzacs slipped away in the darkness, their boots bagged to muffle their footsteps, the lonely campfires burning, the 'ghost guns' rigged to fire unattended in the empty trenches, the paramount sentiment was not that of release from a useless, interminable agony. More often it was a sense of loss, a confession of failure and, somehow, a betrayal of comrades who had fallen.

At the cemeteries, the graves had been tended; the living had knelt to offer their apologies to the dead, and thoughts had dwelt on the cruel ironies of war.

Gallipoli! Gallipoli! Scene of great heroism, desperate friendship and failed purpose. Yet 'Joe Buck' had shed the hayseed and earned his six bob a day.

A simple wooden cross marks the last resting place of fifty-five lost comrades of 2nd Infrantry brigade, at the graveyard on Gallipoli.

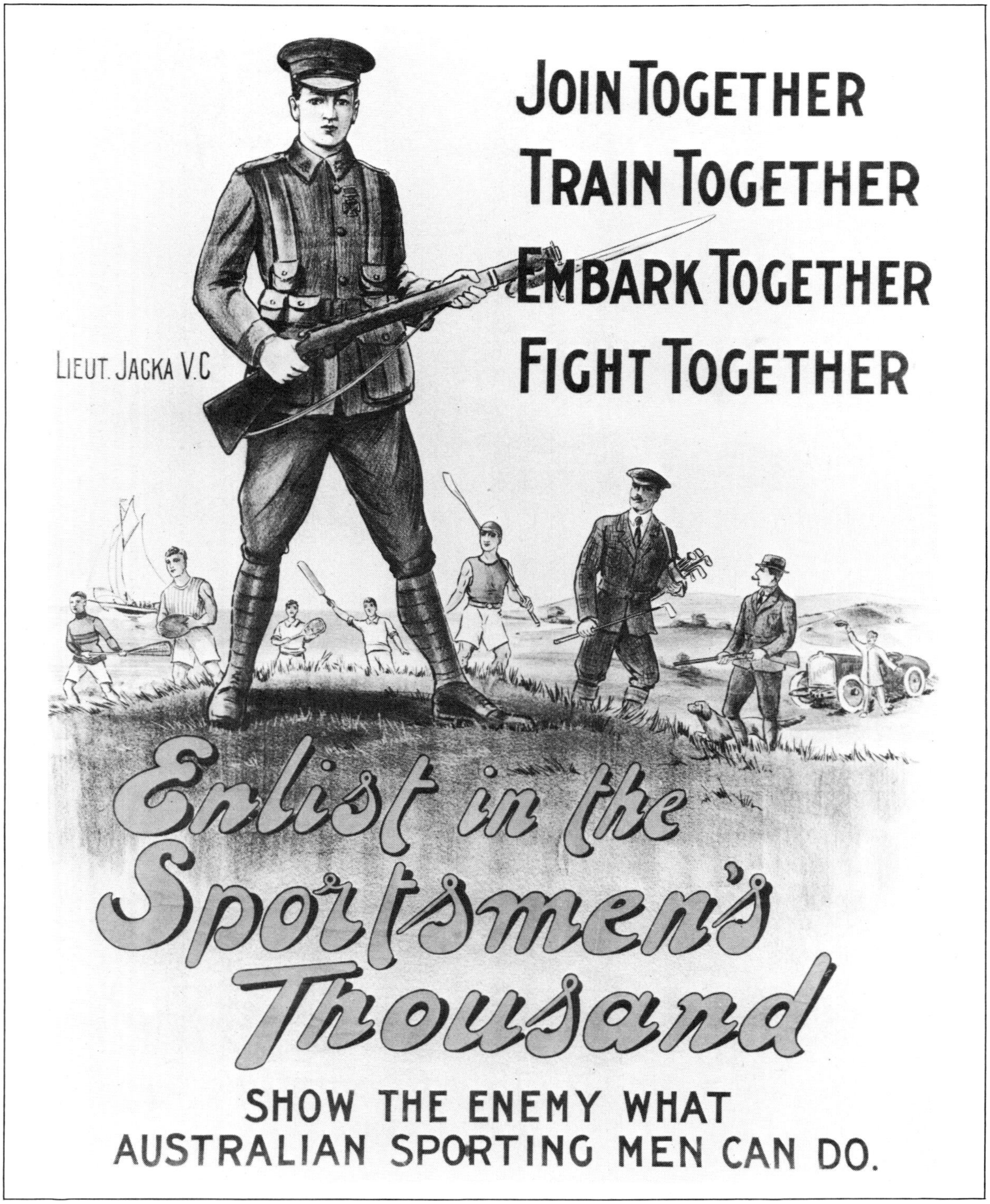
JOIN TOGETHER
TRAIN TOGETHER
EMBARK TOGETHER
FIGHT TOGETHER
LIEUT. JACKA V.C
Enlist in the
Sportsmen's
Thousand
SHOW THE ENEMY WHAT
AUSTRALIAN SPORTING MEN CAN DO.

1916

IN AUSTRALIA, THE CAMPAIGN IN THE Dardanelles had whipped up a new fervour. 'Our boys' were fighting for the Empire! The Turk was experiencing the anger of Australia's brave manhood! The initial phase of the campaign had been accompanied by such bombast that Gallipoli was perceived as some sort of joyous event; there was an exultation that unified the country in the curious illusion of triumph.

Then, when the death lists began to come through, it became apparent that something very different was going on. Even though it was the policy of Britain and the Dominions to exaggerate success and minimize losses, it was hard to hide the fact that sons and brothers and husbands were being slaughtered on those faraway hills. In the first fever of patriotism, recruitment surged. Then, when the sombre picture became clearer, the volunteering waned. Recruitment in July 1915 had reached 36 000, but by November it had slumped to 11 000.

It was left to the politicians and 'patriots' to put fire into the soul, and shame into the heart of the tardy. By 1916, recruitment rallies were visited with a renewed urgency. Britain had introduced conscription in early 1916, and New Zealand was to follow. Canada also was preparing for compulsory military service.

In Australia, enlistment remained – and was to do so throughout the war – a matter of free will, in theory at least.

The term 'shirker' was to become much used. It had shameful connotations, and eligible men not in uniform came to fear it. They were persuaded to duty by a particularly odious breed of women sometimes referred to as 'the Shrieking Sisterhood'. It was the Sisters who maligned indiscriminately, penned the poison letters and allocated the white feathers. What a pity that the theme of sexual equality was not abroad in those days. It would have given the Sisters the opportunity to be soldiers themselves, and charge the machine-guns over mounds of dead.

OPPOSITE: *An appeal to the sporting instinct. Lieutenant Albert Jacka is a hero of Gallipoli whose image is used to encourage others to join in the game of war.*

But the temper of the times demanded that men offer themselves for war, and they did. There was no worry about not being good enough now, no tears from those rejected. Few were. The strict selection procedures that in 1914 culled 'the finest-looking soldiers of the war' had been relaxed. Britain had made it known that it wanted every man Australia could raise. Australia was doing its damnedest to comply.

BY MID-1916, THERE WERE 100 000 Australian and New Zealand troops in France. The first batch – many of them veterans of Gallipoli – had arrived early in the year and been posted around Armentieres. At long last it was possible for the Anzacs to meet Mademoiselle and say 'parlez-vous'!

It was paradise!

For those men who had spent so many long, harrowing months on the wretched, flyblown hills of Gallipoli, there were unbelievable sights: there were waving poplars and spring flowers and green fields; there were houses, farms, rustic villages, quaint streets. And there were colourful people – women and children and old men engaged in the timeless pursuits of rural France as though war had never come, and never would.

'Like a fairyland!' they wrote in letters home. 'Beautiful beyond dreams!'

Even those who had never experienced Gallipoli or war of any kind were captured by it. One boy wrote to his mother: 'France beats about every place for being God's Own Country.'

And not only was France beautiful, its people seemed to love the Anzacs.

'Vive l'Australie!' they shouted, and urged gifts

of food and wine upon them. The Anzacs had come from the other side of the world to fight for La Belle France. And they would be brave soldiers, who would do great things to drive back the Hun!

Even at the Front during those first few months, the conditions were close to heart's desire. The line itself was relatively quiet, and a short stroll away there were canteens and shops where they could buy tobacco and groceries and sweets for very little. There were newspapers from London, and farms where it was possible to barter for eggs or fresh fruit or beer.

And there was also the *estaminet*.

The *estaminets*! Throughout the campaign at the Western Front these inns of many happinesses were to be the solace of thousands of soldiers. There, the six-bob-a-day man could be relieved of his wealth, live it up on beer and champagne and perhaps dally with the girls. Often, the punishment parade followed those rowdy nights. Who cared! This is what a soldier's life was really all about!

For many, that first taste was sweet beyond dreams. Yet it was to prove to be nothing but a fattening for the great feast of 'the Butcher's Picnic'.

THE SOMME OFFENSIVE HAD BEEN planned for many months. Until this stage of the war, France had carried the greatest burden of battle at the Western Front. Now Britain's 'New Army'–those volunteers and conscripts raised in Britain to replace the regular army, which had been all but wiped out–was ready. The 'new chooms' were marshalled to face the Hun, head-on.

The plan was to launch a massive French and British attack on the German lines, assaulting and overrunning the carefully prepared entrenchments that the Germans had been able to establish over many months. This was to be the big breakthrough for the Entente, the turning point of the war. But early in the year, the Alliance pre-empted the plan by launching a massive attack on Verdun, which effectively preoccupied much of the French Army's resources.

The planned Somme offensive, which remains one of the bloodiest battles in world history, was to be conducted primarily by British forces.

The commander of the British Armies in France was General, later Field Marshal, Sir Douglas Haig, a figure of great contention in this war, revered by some, condemned and hated by others. He was a Scot, one of the family of famous whisky distillers, a military man with a long history of distinguished service in the British Army. A precise man, who spoke little, thought deeply and believed implicitly that God was on the Empire's side. At night he would retire to consider the verities contained in the good books–the Bible, *The Pilgrim's Progress*, the book of *Scottish Metric Psalms*. He rarely went near the front lines, declaring that too close an association with the carnage would weaken his resolve and detract from the task allotted to him.

Haig saw the conflict on the Western Front as essentially a contest of will: the side that could persist despite any magnitude of loss, and beyond the limits of exhaustion, would prevail. Men's lives and the force of arms were secondary to the demonstration of a supreme purpose. The philosophy is not new in war; nor, as every military commander knows, is it devoid of truth. But in 1914-18, the credo was more fiercely held to–by both British and German leaders–and more central to tactics than in most great conflicts before or since.

Even before the Battle of the Somme, Haig had told the War Council that British casualties in this demonstration of will could number 500 000. His estimate was to be proved almost exactly right. On the first day alone, 60 000 British troops were to fall.

This was 'the Butcher's Picnic'. The Australians were to share in its bloody celebration.

THE AUSTRALIAN FORCES IN FRANCE HAD been enlarged to four divisions, each made up of a nucleus of Gallipoli veterans, the remainder being volunteers recruited in 1915. Three of the divisions, the First, Second and Fourth, were to undertake an attack on Pozieres, a tactically important village adjoining the British-held sector at Albert. The Fifth Division, along with a British division, was to be engaged in a diversionary attack on Fromelles, not far from Armentieres. This was a sideshow, a feint designed to divert German attention from the more important assaults elsewhere.

For many of the men of the Fifth Division, this was to be the first real taste of war on the Western Front. The veterans from the Dardanelles had told them that 'it couldn't be as bad as Gallipoli'. But in so many ways it was. Even far worse.

The Fifth Division, flanked by the British, penetrated the German lines that day. Then, after a fierce counterattack by the enemy, the flank held by the British faltered. That night, the battlefield of Fromelles was to become a slaughterhouse.

In no-man's-land, amid mounds of dead, the wounded cried out for help. The area was enveloped in such a hail of shell and machine-gun fire that those who attempted to help faced almost certain death.

Negotiations took place with the Germans and a truce was agreed on so that both sides could retrieve their dead and wounded. But when the decision was referred to divisional headquarters, the truce was refused. The Commander-in-Chief decreed that this form of humanitarian arrangement could never be entered into by British forces. To do so would reflect a weakness of will and undermine the determination to crush the enemy.

There was no truce. The lull in the fighting while a decision was awaited suddenly ended as the battlefield was enveloped in a new hail of fire. Dying men were left pitifully abandoned.

The sight of mates in an agony of despair was too great a torture for some soldiers. Out they went, to return with wounded comrades on their backs or dragging them along the ground. Some rescuers died. Others, while performing impossible tasks, were besieged with appeals from more wounded nearby.

'Hey, cobber, don't forget me!'

This is what the soldier's ethic of mateship is all about. The comrade is the first protector, life's last link in the face of death. A terrible reliance, a desperate trust. Old soldiers rarely forget it.

Many men who would otherwise have died at Fromelles were brought to safety that night. But there were hundreds who could not be reached. The sight of mates abandoned at that battle was to become a memory that would haunt the survivors for years to come.

The Fifth Division had been truly blooded at the Western Front. In a single night of fierce fighting, it had sustained 5500 casualties.

FORTY KILOMETRES SOUTH-WEST OF Fromelles, the men of the three divisions of the I ANZAC Corps had been assembled for what was to be tactically the far more important battle of Pozieres. They knew nothing of the experiences of the Fifth Division. Pozieres was to be the first major offensive for most of them. The I ANZAC Corps went into this battle fresh-faced, determined, even with a sense of exultation.

Pozieres was a minor agricultural hamlet, backed by hills where the Germans had become deeply entrenched. British divisions had previously tried and failed to take the village. Most of the buildings had been reduced to ruins, but a number of key German fortifications had withstood the intense artillery fire and remained a severe obstacle to any assault.

Within a matter of days in mid-July, the Australian division had advanced deep into the village of Pozieres and controlled its key sectors. It was a great achievement, a victory that demonstrated the quality of the newly arrived Australian forces in France.

But it was not without its moments of military idiocy.

At the foremost point of the advance, at Dead Man's Road, two Australian colonels reconnoitring amid shellfire and mounds of dead were handed a message marked 'urgent and secret'. It read:

> A number of cases have lately occurred of men failing to salute the Army Commander when passing in his car, in spite of the fact that the car carries his flag upon the bonnet. This practice must cease.

There was little time for saluting before the attack. There was less after victory at the village. The Australians were directed to press their assault, but at the same time the Germans had marshalled a counterattack with troops ordered under threat of court-martial to retake all lost ground.

From then until the end of August, the Anzacs were to carry out some of the most terrible offensives of the war.

The Germans had decided to give full play to the newly developed artillery technique known as the 'creeping barrage'. Lines of attacking troops were met with an incessant rain of shellfire that descended like a wall, either behind the first line of advancing troops, isolating it from its support forces, or ahead of it, acting like a great explosive curtain veiling the German trenches.

These terrible barrages thundered day after day. The landscape became a wasteland. The village of Pozieres was razed, the bricks reduced to dust and great trees blown into tiny splinters. The bodies of men became as nothing.

It seems incomprehensible that soldiers could have fought and advanced and lived. Somehow most did, each according to his own manner and his physical and emotional limits.

Advancing platoons often dealt with frontal curtains of shellfire by holding themselves erect and advancing right through them.

'It was like waiting for your turn at the hotel bar,' one soldier put it. 'Each man was certain to be served in due course.'

Death was so ordinary and freely available that often it ceased to have meaning. The history of the 24th Battalion tells of an officer who came upon four soldiers in a trench playing cards. Their sergeant had just been killed during the game. They had picked up his cards and continued his hand. When the officer returned later, all four were dead.

Some could adapt, at least mentally; others could not. As the advance continued into August, beyond Pozieres and its surrounding heights to Mouquet Farm, the incessant shellfire became too much for the mind to bear. Men went mad. Others turned and ran. Hundreds were seen 'shaking like aspen leaves', their nervous systems all but collapsed.

C. E. W. Bean summed it up:

> The shelling of Pozieres did not merely probe characters and nerve. It left them stark naked as no other experience of the A.I.F. ever did.

Casualties of the three divisions of the ANZAC Corps during July and August were 23 000. With the Fifth Division's losses of 5500 at Fromelles, the Australian force suffered more grievously in six weeks at the Western Front than during eight months at Gallipoli.

Pozieres profoundly changed the Australian soldier's attitude to war. Those who experienced that battle could never again look on it as a game, or accept the methods by which it was then waged.

Yet the Anzacs had proved themselves better than most at persisting in the charnel house of the Somme.

In October, when the Australians were ordered back to that front after a brief rest, there were widespread complaints that the British were asking more of the Australians than of their

The longing for the sunlit days of home. Few Australians who experienced the bitter cold of the Somme winter in 1916 ever forgot that misery.

own. Haig's Chief of Staff, General Kiggell, argued that the best had been selected from those divisions available to the British Army.

'There are certain divisions which if given a thing to do, they do it,' he told the Australian war correspondent Keith Murdoch. '*All* the Australian divisions are in this category.'

Even if they didn't salute.

THE NEWS OF THE TERRIBLE LOSSES ON the Somme added fire to the campaign for a referendum on conscription waged in October 1916. Gallipoli had been a shock to the nation, but the Western Front was proving even more relentless and bloody.

'Death lists'—ghastly slips of paper listing the names of casualties and sold in the streets for a penny each—were now being issued constantly. The cold print offered clear evidence that loved ones, friends and acquaintances were suffering and being sacrificed. In suburban streets, the sight of a clergyman could cause women to hide, terrified he was coming to tell them that someone they loved was lost.

Those for the 'Yes' vote, including the new Prime Minister, Billy Hughes, were strident in their call for compulsory military service in line with Britain and the other Dominions. 'Go to the booth, and by the dagger of your vote destroy the monster of despotism,' he told a rally in Sydney. Many thousands of Australians agreed with him, harbouring the deeply felt sentiment that all able-bodied men, and not just volunteers, should be offered for the Empire's cause. The 'Shrieking Sisterhood' must have had a field day, scavenging in the fowl-houses for white feathers.

But equally emotional factions, notably elements of the Catholic community and Labour movement, were against the proposal. On the eve of the vote, the *Australian Worker* put it: 'To apply compulsion to these men and deprive them of all control over their destinies, is to be guilty of sacrilege against humanity!' Those for the 'No' vote were well aware that it was the women – the mothers, wives and sisters, who feared the loss of their menfolk – who would sway the decision. The anti-conscription leaflet *The Blood Vote* offered doggerel, full of pathos, designed to touch key emotions:

> 'Why is your face so white, Mother?
> Why do you choke for breath?'
> 'O I have dreamt in the night, my son
> That I doomed a man to death.'
>
> 'They gave me the ballot paper,
> The grim death warrant of doom.
> And I smugly sentenced the man to death
> In that dreadful little room.'

Sentiment triumphed over patriotic duty, if only by a slender margin. The 'Yes' vote polled 1 087 000, and the 'No', 1 160 000. Three States – New South Wales, Queensland and South Australia – returned majorities against the proposal.

The soldier vote was interesting, indicating that those at the Front were not overwhelmingly in favour – 72 000 voted 'Yes', but nearly 59 000, 'No'.

Plenty of men who had gone through Gallipoli and Pozieres did not want others forced to share the misery.

1917

THE THIRD YEAR OF THE WAR BEGAN in great gloom. The losses in the Somme offensive and the virtual stalemate on the Western Front had depressed the Australian people. In Britain and France, this mood was far more profound. There seemed no way out, no end in sight to this terrible struggle.

In March the situation worsened, with the overthrow of the Tsar stunting Russian efforts on the Eastern Front. The great fear was that the Russians would collapse altogether, allowing the Alliance to concentrate all its forces on the Western Front. This fear was soon to be realized.

There was one major source of hope: in April, the United States entered the war. America had a population of 100 million and immense industrial power. It had the potential to play the decisive role in Europe, but was not nearly ready to do so. It had to raise its substantial army – from the outset, through a form of conscription – train and equip it, then transport it to Europe. It was estimated, and it proved to be correct, that the United States could not play its full part until mid-1918.

Meanwhile the burden of the war rested with the powerful yet embattled forces of the British Empire and that of France, whose army was already showing signs of dangerous weariness and dissent.

THE AUSTRALIAN DIVISIONS HAD SPENT the winter of 1916-17 in the trenches near Gueudecourt in the Somme region. The conditions were miserable for the soldiers on both sides. Yet no troops found them as unbearable as the Australians.

Every old soldier who served here remembers those times. The cold! The snow coated the ground, and the icy winds found a way through the crevices of any protective cover. Men slept in groups, sharing bodily warmth and the meagre two blankets allocated to each.

Those from the northern areas of Australia, who had never seen snow, found these conditions almost impossible. To some, even Gallipoli, with the flies and stench of bodies, was preferable. At Gallipoli, at least the burning sun had kept the blood circulating.

There were attempts to provide one hot meal a

Hand-knitted balaclavas and thick woollen socks, lovingly made by the ladies of the Australian Comforts Fund, help keep out the aching cold in the Somme trenches.

Tasmanians of the 40th Battalion just out of the line at Bullecourt, May 1917.

day. Some soldiers were lucky, but others, further from the makeshift cookhouses, received theirs semi-chilled. The alternative was tinned food that, when opened, was found to be frozen solid. The bread was so hard it was often impossible to cut and had to be smashed into edible pieces. There was hot tea, but a common water source was an ice-covered shell-hole, occasionally spiced with the corpse of a luckless soldier.

The consolation was that there were regular relief periods behind the lines. Sorrows vanished when the relief order came. Men could find their way to the relative warmth of a station where there were hot meals and tolerably comfortable billets. Sometimes, if a soldier's luck was in, there was the opportunity to visit the nearest village to experience the delights of the *estaminet*.

Ah, the *estaminet*! The soldier's friend in this bugger of a war!

THE 1917 SPRING OFFENSIVE, WITH ITS prospect of bloody battles, was in a sense a relief from the purgatory of that winter. The Germans had staged a tactical retreat to the Hindenburg Line. There, they had entrenched themselves behind earthworks and immense belts of wire linking fortified villages. As part of a major assault by British, Canadian and Australian forces, 1 ANZAC Corps was selected to attack the line around the fortified village of Bullecourt.

The battle known as 'First Bullecourt' is considered a masterpiece of military incompetence. It was authorized by the Commander of the British Fifth Army, General Gough (the man who had insisted on Australians saluting his staff car at Pozieres), against the advice of his senior officers. On 11 April, Australian forces attacked with insufficient artillery cover and over open country in full view of enemy machine-guns. The new weapon of war, the tank, was to be used in this battle. Twelve were to take part, but they arrived

late and then either broke down or were put out of action on the battlefield. First Bullecourt was a miserable failure with one redeeming feature: it was later to be used at staff colleges as an illustration of how not to conduct a battle.

Second Bullecourt, which was scarcely better planned, was a longer and bloodier affair. The attack was renewed on 3 May. Despite fierce German resistance, the Australian, British and Canadian forces broke through the line and Bullecourt finally fell, with the Australians repulsing a massed counterattack by the Third Prussian Guards. Australian losses at the two Bullecourts were 10 000 – 3000 in the first assault, 7000 in the second.

At the end of May, when I ANZAC Corps was withdrawn for its longest rest of the war, the men left the battlefields with some hard things to say about the quality of the British High Command.

But as the 'old Diggers' marched away for the rest they had earned so well, a new breed of

Gas casualties await treatment at a dressing station, Flanders, 1917.

Australian soldiers was emerging at the Front. They were more smartly presented, better disciplined, less unruly. These were the men of the Third Division, who had been based in England during most of 1916, undergoing intensive training. As with the other divisions, there was a core of Gallipoli veterans, but most had had no real experience of war. When they arrived at the Somme late in 1916, the veterans of Lone Pine and Fromelles and Pozieres greeted them with scepticism. The bright-eyed and bushy-tailed men of the Third Division had not had the privilege of being mauled by battle, and they had taken so long to get to the Front they were nicknamed 'The Neutrals'.

The commander of 'The Neutrals' was Major General John Monash. He had been a brigadier at Gallipoli but a part-time soldier before the war. An engineer by profession, he had outstanding

Commander of the Australian Army Corps, Lieutenant General Sir John Monash (from an official portrait).

academic qualifications – Master of Engineering, Master of Laws and Bachelor of Arts. He was noted for his superb intellect, meticulous planning and a healthy regard for his men's welfare. Yet there were serious handicaps in his background. He was Jewish at a time when anti-Semitism was rife, and although he was Australian born, his parents were German.

To some, in those hysterical, unforgiving days, Monash was a Hun.

'The Neutrals' and Monash arrived at the Western Front with much to prove. Both were to have a significant effect on Australia's fortunes in the war.

The Third Division was linked with the New Zealand Division and the British 25th Division in a new grouping, the II ANZAC Corps. The new Corps' first task was to attack the German stronghold at Messines in Flanders. The Germans had occupied strategically important high ground in this area since 1914 and had resisted many attempts to dislodge them. Australian, British and Canadian engineers had been working for two years driving tunnels through to the underside of the ridge. Mines had been laid, and on 7 June a series of immense explosions obliterated many of the enemy's foremost trenches.

The infantry attack that followed was a brilliant success. The II ANZAC Corps had been assigned the southern end of the ridge, including the village of Messines. The Third Division, the New Zealanders and the British 25th Division advanced in one line and, despite some resistance, quickly attained their objective.

Messines was an important victory for the combined British forces. It also had a heartening effect on the Australian side. Monash's 'Neutrals' had faced the first challenge of a major battle and proved themselves every bit as good as the rest.

The significance of Messines was that it enabled Haig to proceed with his major offensive of 1917, the Third Battle of Ypres. Haig had put the plan to the British War Cabinet earlier in the year. He had proposed a huge assault westward towards the sea from Ypres (known to the troops as 'Wipers'). The plan was to scythe through the German forces, either encircling them or driving them out from the Belgian submarine ports, which posed such a threat to the British sea lanes.

The War Cabinet, and in particular the British Prime Minister, Lloyd George, had reservations about Haig's concept of massed assault – especially since the slaughter at the Somme the previous year. There were also well-recognized problems with the Flanders terrain, which drained poorly and was subject to heavy rain, creating miserable conditions for major battles in the region in 1914 and 1915.

Haig's view prevailed. The Cabinet agreed to Third Ypres, with the proviso that it be undertaken with the substantial support of the French forces. The French High Command committed itself to this.

Then, in April and May, the French Army came

dangerously close to collapse. Mutinies were reported in sixty-one divisions. Soldiers refused to take the lines, claiming they were being sacrificed by ruthless and inefficient generals. One hundred and fifty ringleaders were rounded up and sentenced to death, although only twenty-three were executed.

The French withdrew their major infantry support from the Ypres offensive, opting to dig in to give them time to restore morale and to wait for American troops and tanks to arrive at the Western Front. Haig no longer had the French support the War Council had insisted on when approving Third Ypres. But with the success of Messines in mind, the British Commander-in-Chief unilaterally decided to wage the battle with the British forces virtually unaided.

On 31 July, Third Ypres began with a bombardment of colossal power. The thunder of guns could be heard as far away as Dover and even in parts of London. Almost every British division was to be engaged in this appalling battle, which was to be remembered with loathing for years to come by those who took part.

In the Somme region, the veterans of I ANZAC Corps – the men who had taken the full brunt of Australian operations in the war – had benefited from the respite from the conflict. They had been given almost four months to rest and retrain. There had been time to sleep, wander in the villages, fish in the streams, read a book or play cricket. Then there had been training, soundly conducted, not only lifting their physical strength but intelligently enlarging their knowledge of battle. Men who had been sapped by the physical and mental stress of the front lines were transformed. In late July, I ANZAC Corps was moved to GHQ reserve in Flanders in preparation for the later stages of the battle.

Four officers of the 8th Battalion take shelter with their men behind a pillbox in Flanders, October 1917.

The ghostly aftermath of battle. Australians walk a duckboard track bridging shell-holes at Chateau Wood, Ypres Sector, October 1917.

C. E. W. Bean described in the *Official History* how the men of I ANZAC Corps readied themselves for this new battle:

> . . . the troops had seen too much hard fighting to welcome the prospect of more. Yet as the day came for marching to the forward areas, there came over them a marked eagerness. Each man had faced up to whatever private problems this battle had in store for him. There flew around the messes grim jokes as to who should inherit his old friend's boot or binoculars and despite all the old dreads and horrid memories, men were obviously keen to put into use the drill they had been practising, and confident they could outplay the enemy. The excitement of the great game, mingled with other feelings.

In September, after a lull in the Third Battle of Ypres, I ANZAC Corps went in to join II ANZAC Corps in the great thrust eastward. Until October, the fighting was marked with success, with a series of advances through Polygon Wood, the Menin Road, Broodseinde. The fighting was bitter, some of it involving hand-to-hand combat and the clearance of concrete emplacements from which the German machine-gunners had to be routed with the utmost ruthlessness.

It is easy to be glib about battle and to dwell on heroism and soldierly virtues. But the savagery of war also generates great ugliness. Bean offers a picture – and a justification – of what fierce fighting is all about.

> Most men are temporarily half-mad, their pulse pounding at their ears, their mouths dry, the noblest among them are straining their wills to keep a cool head, the less self-controlled are for the time being governed by primitive impulse. With death singing about their ears they will kill till they grow tired of killing. When they have been wracked by machine-gun fire the routing out of enemy troops is almost inevitably the signal for a butchery at least of the first few who emerge, and even the helpless wounded may not be spared. It is idle to cry shame upon such incidents unless he cries out upon the whole system of war for this frenzy is an inevitable condition in desperate fighting. The nobler the leaders, the more they endeavour to mitigate the futile ruthlessness, but ruthlessness is a quality essential in hand-to-hand fighting, and soldiers were deliberately trained to it . . .

This form of merciless fighting continued until 4 October, when the British forces were at the outskirts of the village of Passchendaele. At last a great victory seemed possible. The objectives set for the Third Battle of Ypres seemed attainable, and German resistance appeared to be failing.

Then down came the rain.

It began as a drizzle on 4 October and a few days later had developed into a deluge. The ground, torn apart by shellfire, became a quagmire. Men were captured by mud, sometimes waist-deep. Shell-holes filled with water, and soldiers drowned in them. Guns would not fire because of rain or mud. It became almost impossible to move heavy artillery. In one case, a team of men took seventeen hours to position a gun, a task that normally would have taken one hour.

Haig's senior commanders urged a pause or even a cessation of the attack, but the Commander-in-Chief refused. He insisted the Germans were on the brink of collapse and that a great effort would break them. The assault on the Passchendaele region continued in conditions almost beyond imagining.

Monash's 'Neutrals' and the New Zealanders were ordered to take the village of Passchendaele. Somehow they went forward, a few entering the outskirts only to be driven back by machine-guns or exhaustion or the German gas that seared the throat and lungs, disabling some men for the rest of their lives. When soldiers came out of the lines, their faces were described as being 'like those of dead men'.

In early November, the Canadians finally broke through and took Passchendaele, an extraordinary feat, but too late. The bloodbath of Third Ypres had ended. British casualties in the

TOP: *The scene on the Menin Road, September 1917.* BOTTOM: *Wounded men of the 8th Battalion on the Menin Road, 1917. The man walking with his arm in a sling is the regimental medical officer.*

TOP: *The absolute devastation of the village of Bapaume after capture by the Australians in 1917.*
BOTTOM: *A German corpse (foreground) acts as companion to Australians, living and dead, in a railway cutting during the battle of Passchendaele, October 1917.*

Flanders campaign were 440 000 – 38 000 of them Australian.

Passchendaele, observed the British historian Liddell Hart, had become 'a name of ill-omen and a synonym for military barrenness'.

1918

IN AUSTRALIA AT THE BEGINNING OF 1918, the possibility of this terrible war ever ending seemed to be slipping away. The awful losses in Flanders – worse than at the Somme in 1916 – had cast a pall over the whole country. There was hardly a family that had not been touched by tragedy. The maimed were filling the hospitals, and in the streets of towns and cities there were men without arms or legs, men blind or hoarse from the effects of gas, many who were clearly emotionally broken.

It was all so different from what had been expected in those buoyant days of 1914 when 'the originals' had marched off, bound for glory in the cause of Empire.

A second conscription referendum had been held in December 1917, and the proposal had again been narrowly defeated. The Prime Minister, Billy Hughes, had campaigned fiercely and at one meeting had been pelted with eggs. (He had promptly punched one of the throwers, causing an all-in brawl.) But Hughes and his Cabinet, although urging more soldiers for the Front, were also desperately concerned about the way the men were being used. Australian forces were employed as instruments of the British Army, not as a national fighting force, making it more difficult politically to protect them against the profligacy of the High Command.

Hughes wanted an Australian Army. Haig had refused, because Australia did not have the number of men – more than 200 000 – to create such a major fighting unit. Hughes pressed for the next best thing: an Australian Army Corps. He was to have more success in achieving this.

In Britain, the nationalistic aims of Australia did not make much sense at all, at least to the general public. It had been the High Command's policy to make no specific reference to colonial forces in reports of fighting, defining all achievements as simply 'British'. The leading London newspapers scarcely indicated that the Australians – or the Canadians or New Zealanders – were involved in the conflict at all.

Yet, although the High Command did not publicly acknowledge the colonial effort, it was to depend on the Dominions' soldiers more and more. The huge drafts of men that had been chewed up by the battles of the Somme and Third Ypres – almost a million troops – had appalled the British Cabinet. Lloyd George loathed Haig and longed to sack him. But Haig had the support of the generals and of the King, who had immense powers of persuasion. Lloyd George's recourse was to starve Haig's five armies of reserves, allocating new troops to other fronts or keeping them in the United Kingdom. Many British divisions, already weakened by losses of their finest officers and men in the fighting since 1914, were a shadow of the effective fighting forces they had once been.

In 1918, it became the habit, if not the declared policy, of the British High Command, to rely more and more on select divisions that had proved their capacity for attack. These included the elite Guards divisions, the Scots and the colonial forces of Canada, New Zealand and Australia.

The test came late in March 1918. Germany, after signing a peace agreement with the Bolsheviks, had a million additional troops released from the Russian Front. It was the Alliance's final attempt to turn the tide. The plan was to split the British and French Armies and to wheel onto the British Armies and crush them.

On 21 March, the main attack fell on the Fifth British Army at St Quentin in the Somme region. In three days the line had broken, and the Fifth

A captured German stronghold, the corrugated iron riddled with shrapnel.

Army was in retreat. It was the most serious crisis on the Western Front since the battle of the Marne in 1914.

Soon after, Field Marshal Haig made his famous appeal to the troops:

> Every position must be held to the last man; there must be no retirement. With our backs to the wall and believing in the justice of our cause, each one of us must fight on to the end.

Australian divisions had been moved into the front lines in the Somme region. The roads were so jammed with civilians and retreating troops that it was difficult to move men and equipment forward.

A French woman watched a group of Australians marching to the front and observed:

'Not much salute, march all over the road, officers talk with the men . . . but good soldiers.'

A British artillery officer commented:

'They were the first cheerful, stubborn people I had met in retreat.'

The First Division was diverted to the River Lys area, where in the Nieppe Forest they put up a crucial resistance to a German advance towards the Channel ports.

A series of attacks and counterattacks in the Somme region made battlegrounds famous: Dernancourt, Morlancourt Ridge, Hangard Wood, Villers-Bretonneaux. By the end of April, when the German thrust had been exhausted, four Australian divisions held half the British line, sixty-one kilometres of Front from Amiens to the French emplacements.

Australians had not stopped the German offensive alone, but as Bean understates, there had been 'special value in their presence'. Their central achievement was preventing the Germans from reaching their main objective: the vital rail centre of Amiens.

There was a new spirit amongst the Australian soldiers now. The fighting was not like that at Fromelles or Pozieres or Passchendaele. There seemed to be a purpose in what they were doing, and they were seen to be doing it well. And they were commanded in a different way.

In March, the British had finally agreed to the integration of the five Australian divisions – 166 000 men – into the Australian Army Corps. It was led by Lieutenant General Sir John Monash, former commander of the derided 'Neutrals', the Jewish part-time soldier with German ancestry.

In many ways, Monash was to prove the best weapon ever placed at the Australian soldier's disposal. He was a brilliant organizer and a man of great character, who preached the unusual dictum that officers were not the masters of soldiers but their servants. Troops could not be thrown at enemy guns like missiles. Their leaders had the responsibility of setting attainable objectives and, through planning, ensuring that success was achieved with the least possible loss. Monash's philosophy of battle is indicative of the man:

> A perfected modern battle plan is like nothing so much as a score for an orchestral composition where the various arms and instruments, and the tasks they perform are their respective musical phrases. Every individual unit must make its entry precisely at the proper moment, and play its phrase in the proper harmony . . .

Monash's concept of a battle as a concert was put into effect in July with the attack on the village of Hamel. It was a relatively minor action, relying largely on tanks and involving only three brigades. But men and machinery were used together in a way not previously seen in this war. The tanks were not only attack units but also carriers of ammunition, taking over the work of hundreds of soldiers. Aircraft did not merely reconnoitre, they parachuted weapons and supplies to forward areas. The troops were advanced in stages to set lines. From there, a fresh wave moved through to continue the assault to a further defined line. The element of surprise was essential.

The battle of Hamel was staged on 4 July 1918, with 2000 newly arrived American troops joining the Australians. It was all over in ninety-three minutes. All objectives were attained. Casualties were negligible.

Hamel was to be described as 'the first modern battle of the Great War'.

Monash's plans for Hamel were published and circulated to senior commanders throughout the British Army. This was a new way to run a war. Successful battles were not measured by a count of the corpses or the degree of exhaustion on either side. They required the orchestration of men and arms, creating a harmony where before there had been a cacophony of slaughter and despair.

The experiences of Hamel influenced the conduct of the great British offensive of August 1918. This was the 'big push' of the year – the successor to the Somme of 1916 and Third Ypres of 1917, where great attacks had been carried out with terrible consequences. This time it was to be different.

On 8 August, the British Fourth Army, spearheaded by the Australian and Canadian Corps, struck at the German lines to the north of Amiens. The attack, perfectly planned, went through swiftly and easily.

It was a great victory.

'August 8 was the black day for the German army in this war,' the German General Ludendorff wrote, adding, 'the war must be ended.'

Later, behind the lines at Villers-Bretonneaux, Australian, British and Canadian generals assembled to celebrate and to congratulate one another on the most bloodless victory of any of the great battles. Field Marshal Haig made one of his rare visits to the Front to address them.

There he was: the commander of five armies

The once impregnable Hindenburg Line is crossed by Australian forces, October 1918.

and 2 million men, the man of steel, the apostle of bloody attrition, the generalissimo some saw as being so bereft of feeling for human life that they called him 'The Butcher'.

'You do not know what the Australians and the Canadians have done for the Empire in these days,' he began.

Then he stopped, choking on his words. And he wept.

But at the Front, the Anzacs were under strain, too. They had achieved a string of astonishing successes – at Mont St Quentin, the Hindenburg Line, Peronne – pressed to the limit, always in the front line; fierce fighters who had come to be used as shock troops. But they were changing.

The Americans were appearing in force at the Western Front now. An Australian correspondent saw them and wrote that he felt as though he had 'passed amongst ghosts'. For the Americans were the reincarnation of the Anzacs as they were in the early days in Australia and in Egypt: fresh-faced boys, tall and confident, eager for the experience of battle, immortal.

Perhaps some of the Anzacs would have looked at the Americans and thought the same thing. But they were no longer like that. They were tired; they felt they were being asked to do more than their fair share; they'd had enough. When losses forced battalions to be broken up, some soldiers had refused battle orders unless they could continue to fight with their mates. In another incident, a battalion just returned from the line mutinied when ordered to go back. One hundred and nineteen men were sentenced to ten years in Dartmoor (but, mercifully, were released in 1919).

Prime Minister Billy Hughes, then in France, demanded that all Australian troops be withdrawn for rest. The war, for most Australians at the Western Front at least, was over.

IN 1914, WHEN THE 'ORIGINALS' WENT OFF to war, they left as innocents. Those who came back were different men. They had survived the thunder of the guns, seen the battlefields littered with the bodies of their fellows, learnt the soldierly skills of the slaughterman fulfilling the quota of the day.

The war was a towering experience which took the lives of many, scarred others in mind or in body and left few unchanged in their attitudes towards themselves and to life itself.

But there were virtues, too. Before the war, Australia could hardly have called itself a nation. It was a mere collection of States, newly formed into a Commonwealth but without a true national identity. The Great War changed that. The experiences of Gallipoli, the Middle East and the Western Front united not only soldiers at war but the people at home. It was Australia's war, not just the concern of some State or outpost of the continent. It was Australia's will – no matter how anachronistic some motives might now appear – that was being expressed at the battlefields far away.

Australia's contribution to the Empire's cause had singular aspects: the Australian soldiers were the tallest, the best paid, perhaps the loudest-mouthed and, with the New Zealanders, from the lands farthest removed from the scene of conflict. They were also the only army of volunteers, and they fell more thickly than any others of the British forces. The list of battle casualties tells the story: Canada 51 per cent, United Kingdom 52 per cent, New Zealand 58 per cent and Australia 68 per cent.

The Australians were front-line troops, committed and effective, whose achievements and sacrifices, particularly at the Western Front, were never recognized to the degree they deserved.

Ironically, their worth was acknowledged by the enemy. Field Marshal Hindenburg, Commander of the German Armies, observed that the elite of the British Army were the men from the colonies.

The British Prime Minister, Lloyd George, declared:

'In the annals of all military history, the world has never seen such a fighting force as the AIF.'

But whatever the opinion held by others, the Anzacs knew they had done well. They had taken part in the great spectacle and shown themselves as good as, and sometimes better than, the rest.

Few people recall the Great War now. Anzac Day is commemorated mainly in terms of Gallipoli, but the thoughts of the old soldiers, those few who are left, tend to dwell on the fields and villages of Flanders or France. They remember the one thing that brought dignity and meaning to the whole dirty business: the precious comradeship.

Angela Moody, an old lady of the Melbourne suburb of Brighton, recalls seeing, as a young girl, two soldiers walking together in a Melbourne street. One had been grievously wounded and his head was bandaged, probably concealing a tin plate. After a few steps he would stop and let out a piercing scream, prompted by either some image or a vibration that speared the brain. Others in the street stood back, or looked away.

But it was the second soldier who was so impressive. He held his companion's arm, stopping when he did, waiting for each storm to pass, and then the two moved slowly on.

The patience shown by one man to another was so striking that Angela Moody said:

'I think they must have been brothers.'

They were. Whether by blood or shared experience, they had a kinship. They had endured war, learnt the desperate reliance upon each other, lived through moments so vivid that those not there could never understand. Mateship – the enduring emotion, a sort of love.

'Hey, cobber, don't forget me!'

THE TALE OF TWO GUNNERS

IT'S EARLY 1979 AT THE MELBOURNE offices of the big advertising agency Monahan Dayman Adams. Geoff Burrowes, the agency's recently appointed Planning Director, is hard at work at his desk, minding his own business.

He's visited by God.

On this day, He has taken the guise of Phillip Adams – advertising genius, a principal of Monahan Dayman Adams, public figure, master raconteur and, through print and television, a regular purveyor of Sermons from the Mount.

God spake:

'Geoff, you've got to get in here and monster a bloke called Dixon.'

'What's he done?' asks Burrowes.

'Buggered a commercial,' God-in-the-guise-of-Adams replies. 'He's jacking up because we say he's got to redo it at his expense.'

God adds with great relish:

'Get in there and bash him up for us, Geoff.'

Smart operator, Geoff. Mid-thirties, fast talker, eager beaver. He hasn't the foggiest idea what this is all about, but he recognizes the call from On High when he hears it.

He's taken to the Throne Room, where the archangels of Monahan Dayman Adams are foregathered, sipping iced water and other ingredients. They are looking into the middle distance. There is the subtle intimation of pain.

John Dixon is there, too. Different type. In his fifties, rumpled, no frills, not given to the unnecessary phrase. As chairman of Cambridge Films, he's been around the traps. In fifteen years he's made thousands of commercials. Never before has he been asked to remake one where, as he sees it, the fault lies not in the making but in the agency script.

The iced water tinkles in the glasses clutched by the archangels. Dixon crouches over a tinny, giving the impression of one who has arrived at 'a position'.

Burrowes, a stripling in the advertising business, is going to 'bash him up'.

'Tell him what's going to happen, Geoff,' God-in-the-guise-of-Adams intones.

Quick as a flash, Burrowes sits himself beside Dixon.

'Well, old mate, it's like this,' he says. 'You and I are going to get together and remake this commercial . . .'

Dixon observes Burrowes.

'. . . and how's it going to be done?' he asks.

Good point! Burrowes doesn't know a thing about the commercial: its content, its client, the budget or the reason for discontent. But God and the archangels are looking on, fascinated.

A quick, figurative race to the lip of the precipice. A survey of the depths, then back to the questions.

'To tell the truth, old mate,' Burrowes says, 'I haven't actually wrapped my mind around that yet.'

Then he gives Dixon a winning smile.

'Why don't we just go off somewhere and talk about it?'

In such manner are great unions formed under the aegis of the Almighty.

Needless to say, the commercial is remade. Dixon's worries about cost are (almost) satisfactorily resolved. And Burrowes and Dixon talk and find an unexpected affinity.

There's a notable polarity of personalities here. There's Burrowes: whiz-kid, graduate economist, former personal assistant to Hector Crawford, private secretary to a Federal Minister for the Media, and now an acolyte of the Almighty himself.

There's one other thing: he's a 'gunner'. He's 'gunner be a film producer'. He has this great idea for a movie called *The Man from Snowy River*. No script, but a passionately held idea impelled by a long-standing love affair with the High Plains of Victoria and the images of Banjo Paterson's durable poem.

Dixon is from a different mould. He's very much the veteran craftsman, with a history stretching back to the early days of Australian television. He's learnt his trade at Channel 7 in Melbourne–news, documentaries, many episodes as director of the almost-forgotten *Consider Your Verdict*. Then out in the big wide world as a producer of documentaries and commercials through Cambridge. He's also got odd outside interests. He's a military buff: military history. He's a member of the Council of the Australian War Memorial. What's more, he holds the rank of lieutenant colonel in the Army Reserve.

One day they're talking and Dixon broaches the subject of a television project he's long been wanting to get off the ground. It's about a war–the 'Great One'; the terrible conflict that shook the world in 1914-18.

Problem.

There are few people around whose past indicates less sympathy for matters military than Burrowes. In the 1960s and early 1970s, during the heady days of the anti-Vietnam movement, he'd gone to war against war. At Monash University, when the students had united in noisy revolution, he'd been a sort of King Kong of the *enfants terribles*: radical activist, rabid Marxist, Maoist, Gang of Fourist. He'd been in on all the student insurrections; waved the banners at the forefront of the marches; driven the university administrators crazy. He'd achieved the stunning distinction of being twice expelled from Monash (on each occasion, miraculously managing to get the sentence revoked).

Burrowes looks at Dixon, eyes glazing.

'Tell us about the war, John,' he says.

And Dixon does. As Burrowes recounts, it is one of the most lucid summations of a difficult subject he has ever heard. Dixon talks about 1914 and the little country called Australia that got all excited about an immense yet inscrutable argument that had overtaken Europe. He tells about the young men who besieged the recruiting offices, longing to get into the fight; how they went off, in British eyes, as a bunch of lousy soldiers. Dixon talks about Gallipoli, that proud, tragic fiasco, but dwells on the heart-rending experiences of the Western Front: the trenches and the machine-guns and the thunder of the artillery barrages that shook the earth. Then, how it had become clear that they weren't lousy soldiers at all, but exceptional warriors, fighting and dying, yet holding together through the desperate ethic of mateship in circumstances that defied true description.

The stories go on over many days, Dixon talking, Burrowes taking it in. He knows a lot about Vietnam; he's red-hot on the follies of war. But he hasn't heard the deeds of the old soldiers talked about like this. He's deeply impressed.

'You could have the makings of a great series.'

'I'm no good at the paperwork,' Dixon replies. 'I need a producer.'

Burrowes trots out a few names, but Dixon shakes his head.

TOP: *Producer Geoff Burrowes on location.* BOTTOM: *(left to right) Geoff Burrowes, John Dixon and Director George Miller in discussion during the making of* ANZACS.

'How about you?' Dixon says.

Burrowes finds himself confessing that he's not a producer. He's never produced anything. He's a 'gunner'. ('I've got this idea for a great movie called *The Man from Snowy River*. It's gunner . . .')

'I'm a gunner, too,' Dixon butts in. 'I'm gunner get the story written; I'm gunner direct it, too. Why don't you come in with me as producer and we'll show them we're gunner do it?'

And so it came about . . .

Soon after, 'Gunner' Burrowes hands in his uniform at Monahan Dayman Adams and moves in with 'Gunner' Dixon at Cambridge Films. They are going to shoot a war . . .

But how?

The biggest burden is on Burrowes. Dixon is a walking encyclopaedia on the Great War, but Burrowes has only the bones of it. The first task is to catch up on C.E.W. Bean. Bean was the official war correspondent, and his six volumes of the *Official History* are a masterpiece of fact and observation. A superb literary work. It took thirty years to write and runs to a million words.

There are other tomes covering facets of Australian military activities, volumes dealing with the political, economic and social circumstances prevailing in Australia at the time. Then there's the reading necessary to understand the genesis of the war itself and the involvement of the major powers – Britain, Germany, France, Russia, the United States, Turkey. Scores of books; a sea of words.

There's one important volume Burrowes and Dixon paid close attention to: Patsy Adam-Smith's recently published *The ANZACS*. It's a fine work, which vividly portrays Australia's part in the war from Gallipoli to the Western Front, using the reminiscences and insights of the old soldiers.

Patsy Adam-Smith has shown her worth as both writer and historian. She also has feminine perceptions that Burrowes and Dixon recognize as invaluable in curbing any tendency for the series to become a 'macho romp'. She's brought in as story consultant.

Carpenters cover the walls of the biggest room at Cambridge with whiteboard. Dixon, Burrowes and Adam-Smith set to work with the graffiti – column after column detailing the countries involved and the political circumstances applying in Europe and Australia before, during and after the Great War. Everything is exhaustively cross-referenced.

Then it is the soldiers' turn. What sort of men were they? What were their backgrounds, motivations, aspirations, strengths and weaknesses? There has to be a group around whom the drama can be structured – real people, whose lives and experiences can be moulded to fictional form.

ANZACS must not be just a history lesson. It has to be taut, believable drama, involving characters that audiences care deeply about.

The models are found in the ranks of the 8th Battalion, First Division, a unit enlisted from city and country areas of Victoria. The 8th Battalion was at Gallipoli and served with distinction at the Western Front.

The Battalion's war diary and Nominal Roll are located, and a day-by-day account of its activities throughout the war period emerges. Suddenly there are faces: the soldiers, the NCOs, the officers, the headquarters staff, the nurses. By reading and re-reading the lists of names, occupations and origins, and by charting their fortunes through the Battalion's history, personalities begin to take shape. Key characters 'live', and their relationships, actions and attitudes one to the other are defined. The bones of television drama take shape.

It's an exciting, challenging and engrossing task, with great rewards.

'Never in my life have I worked so hard,' says Burrowes. 'Never in my life have I worked so well.'

It takes a year to master the mass of detail and shape the dramatic structure for sixteen hours of television. A labour of love. It has to be: the three are sustained by a $19 000 development grant from Film Victoria. Over the year that's about $125 a week each.

They've got the shape. Now it's a matter of selling the idea to the television networks – essential if the project is to have any chance at all. Burrowes's exceptional marketing skills are employed. He and Dixon finance a lavish and hugely expensive written and visual display extolling the virtues of the series ('bigger than *War and Peace*, cost equal to the national debt'). Three networks are approached, and top executives look and listen.

Ambitious idea. Beautifully presented. But Burrowes and Dixon? Never heard of them . . .

Each network turns them down flat.

It's *ANZACS'* first foray into the commercial world. It experiences disastrous defeat.

Meanwhile there's been some 'movement at the station'. Burrowes has commissioned the talented actor-writer Fred 'Cul' Cullen to write up Burrowes's idea for a film based on Banjo Paterson's poem 'The Man from Snowy River'. The first draft convinces the resilient Burrowes that he's got the material to make a film.

'It's tough about *ANZACS*, John,' he tells Dixon, 'but I have to get *Snowy* moving. What about you?'

Dixon thinks about it.

'I might knock out a few episodes for the series.'

Burrowes protests: 'But nobody wants it, and you've no credentials as a screen writer.'

'I'll do it anyhow,' says Dixon.

So Burrowes starts work on *Snowy*, seeking backers and working with Cullen on the script. But there's a problem: Cul Cullen is not only a good writer, he's a formidable personality, best characterized by the plumber he plays in a television commercial, who gargles a disinfectant strong enough to clear drains. Burrowes wants changes in the script. The redoubtable Cullen disagrees. They reach an impasse. It's Burrowes's first movie, and he sees himself in danger of losing control of it from the outset.

One day Dixon lopes in with a wad of paper under his arm.

'I've drafted a couple of hours of *ANZACS*,' he announces.

Burrowes is reserved. Great bloke, John. Terrific ideas. Good director. But no screen writer.

Burrowes reads the scripts – and almost falls off his chair. The best first drafts he's read in his life. Real characters; a true feel for story-line. You can 'see' the pictures.

Burrowes is so impressed he asks Dixon to write up some scenes for *Snowy*. Again a marvellous result, and Burrowes hands the entire Cullen script over to Dixon. And gets the results he's looking for.

The Man from Snowy River becomes the most successful Australian film ever released on the home market and goes on to lucrative international distribution.

'Gunners' Dixon and Burrowes have not just gained their stripes in the movie business, they've won commissions in the field.

Not only does *The Man from Snowy River* become a huge money-spinner in the cinemas, it is hot property as a prospective television release. The Australian commercial networks – which rejected the *ANZACS* proposal – bid spiritedly for the rights to show it.

It goes to Kerry Packer's Channel 9, and – to the great satisfaction of Burrowes and Dixon – at a whopping price.

Burrowes rings Kerry Packer, Nine's undisputed overlord. He points out that Nine has paid through the nose for *Snowy* and suggests it's time to look again at *ANZACS* and get in on the ground floor. Packer agrees to a meeting, and Burrowes and Dixon fly to Sydney.

There's no high-powered presentation this time. They meet Packer alone and carry a single sheet of paper describing the idea. Packer doesn't even read it. He puts his feet on the desk, and they talk for an hour. The deal is done.

'Kerry's a great Australian,' says Burrowes. 'A big man. He knows it, and he lets you know it. But there's not an ounce of bullshit in him.'

There's agreement on sales price and development funds, and the deal is sealed with a handshake.

'Want a bit of paper?' asks Burrowes.

'Nope,' says Packer.

'Bloody amazing,' recalls Dixon later.

But that's the way the deal is done.

They've got their first real money. Now they've got to deliver. First by producing top-quality scripts for a series brought back to thirteen hours. It's got to work on paper, not only for an Australian audience but for an overseas market as well.

Burrowes, Dixon and their Associate Producer, Dennis Wright, agree that they need a top writer to come in and look at the work already done on the story outlines. They can't afford any self-indulgence or jingoism in their scripts. They have to be objectively assessed – torn apart if need be. But who could they get? Who's the best possible writer for the job?

Dixon, Burrowes and Dennis Wright sit down and play a little game. They have *carte blanche.* Each jots down a name. Three pieces of paper lie on the desk. Each bears the name 'James Mitchell'. James Mitchell, creator of *Callan, When the Boat Comes In* and many other superbly crafted plays. He is one of the best television writers in the English-speaking world. And he lives in England.

'We'd never get him to come out here and work for a penny-ante lot like us,' protests Burrowes.

Dennis Wright offers a lateral thought.

'Why don't you ring up and ask him?'

With trembling hand, Burrowes picks up the phone and negotiates with Mitchell's agent. Then he rings Mitchell direct.

Voilà! Mitchell's on his way to Australia.

James Mitchell is not only a great writer, he has an exceptional historian's grasp of the First World War. He knows what the Tommies went through; he understands the British political and military ethos. He has a fine understanding of what British audiences will accept or reject in a series that could tend to be jingoistic and underrate Britain's momentous role in that conflict. One of Mitchell's memorable characters is ex-Sergeant Jack Ford of *When the Boat Comes In*. Ford is an ex-Tommy who knows the trenches and is blunt in defence of what his comrades did.There's a lot of Ford in James Mitchell.

Burrowes and Dixon have asked for tough observations, and they get them. The story-line is strengthened, and the characters are given more vigorous dimension.

Mitchell goes off to write three episodes. Dixon takes five. They need another writer.

It's Mitchell who suggests a New Zealander who used to deliver groceries to his London home in the early 1970s. Mitchell has forgotten the young expatriate's career in purveyancing, but he has noted his superb talent for comedy in his subsequent trade as a writer. This is John Clarke, known to Australians and New Zealanders as Fred Dagg, and co-writer of the much-praised Paul Cox film *Lonely Hearts.*

Clarke is offered the job of scripting for *ANZACS.* He accepts like a shot.

At last, after three years of delay and disappointment, John Dixon's great dream of bringing the ANZAC story to life looks like being attained. The typewriters are afire. Before long there are thirteen hours of television on Burrowes's desk. They've done it. It's finally on paper.

Burrowes goes through it all and says:

'John, let's go for a walk.'

The two of them – Starsky and Hutch, great mates, once such opposites in their views on war, now both passionately committed to the deeds of the old soldiers – stroll in the park.

Burrowes drops his bombshell.

'It doesn't work, mate. We've got to do it all over again.'

Dixon looks at him, a man felled.

'What do you mean?' he says.

'Too long; we've lost the thread. We've got thirteen long statements when we can make it shorter and do it better.'

Dixon has poured his heart and soul into the structure and the writing. It's taken part of his life. Now Burrowes is telling him they're back to square one.

It's a measure of the relationship that blows are not struck. Dixon respects Burrowes's judgment, and Dixon is the good soldier. Maybe he's heard of Robert the Bruce.

Off they go again. This round of rewrites takes another year. It's not a matter of stapling episodes – it's a major reconstruction. The whole rhythm of character, plot and subplot has to be altered. Scenes from the scripts of all three writers are blended into single episodes. Fresh scenes are devised to bridge areas where changes have been made. Some of Dixon's favourite moments are bloodily excised.

At the newly established Burrowes-Dixon offices in South Melbourne, there are alarming moments: voices raised; colourful phrases; the grunts and moans of mortal combat and the forebodings of the end of a beautiful friendship.

'We were sure the partnership was over,' Bill Regan, John Dixon's partner, recalls. 'We thought blood was going to flow.'

Burrowes says: 'John and I understand each other.'

Dixon observes: 'Purely a matter of differences in interpretation. Nothing personal.'

Such are the mysteries of the creative process – and why those involved in it often yearn for the blessed simplicities of digging a road, or taming a lion.

But it happens. One day, that harmony of contrasts, 'Gunners' Burrowes and Dixon, emerge from the cloisters, eyes bloodshot, faces pale. Smiling.

ANZACS is ready for the battlefields. It's all there on paper.

The writing's no longer on the wall.

THE BATTLE OF PLEURISY PLAINS

IT'S A COOL AUTUMN DAY AT Beveridge, fifty-six kilometres north of central Melbourne. This is Sleepy Hollow, a little hamlet tucked into the valley adjoining the Hume Highway linking Melbourne and Sydney.

Pam Starbuck has lit the fire, her two young children are at play, and the farmhouse windows frame the rolling hillsides, reflecting that special sense of peace associated with God's little acre.

Then there's an alien sound. It's distant at first, but suddenly it intensifies, to reveal itself as the urgent stutter of a helicopter in swift descent. Suddenly the helicopter is skimming the Starbuck home. The windows rattle, the children cry out, and the tranquillity of the countryside is threatened by Apocalypse Now.

Through the window, Pam Starbuck watches in disbelief. There's the helicopter sweeping low over the adjoining fields. The sheep scatter, the grass bows in rolling waves. Backwards and forwards the helicopter goes, scudding over the far hills, then returning to dart and hover and wheel like a hornet in crisis.

What's a mother, alone with her children, aged ten and six, to make of an event like this? Is there an escapee loose in the area whom the police are attempting to flush out? Has some maniac chosen this spot to practise his version of helicopter wheelies?

Not quite. It's John Dixon looking for the Somme. And he's found it.

A big moment, this. For months, Dixon, Burrowes and Production Designer Les Binns have been scouring Victoria for the spot that could best represent the great killing grounds of the First World War. It's not easy to find anywhere in Australia. The location has to be convincing as France, Belgium, areas of Gallipoli and western Victoria as well. It's Dixon, with his soldier's background, who has recognized the spot that fills the bill exactly: the rolling, almost treeless hills of the Starbuck property at Beveridge.

A few days after the helicopter incident, Pam Starbuck, her husband, David, and his father, David Starbuck senior, who jointly own the 486 hectare sheep and cattle property, receive two visitors. They are Bill Regan, Production Supervisor for *ANZACS*, and Les Binns. They have a proposition that, in general terms, goes something like this:

'Would you mind if we used your paddocks to wage the First World War?'

It's the lifeblood of the entertainment business – the good one-liner.

After the Starbucks have picked themselves up from the floor ('There *did* seem something odd about it at the time,' David Starbuck junior recalls), it transpires that they don't mind at all. Most acceptable arrangements are worked out with Burrowes and Dixon, the 2000 sheep and 100 or so head of cattle are sold off or moved to adjoining pastures, and *ANZACS* moves in.

Beveridge is central to success. The *ANZACS* budget is big – at this stage, $6 500 000 – but so are the ambitions for the series, in terms of size

Production Designer Les Binns checks out the trenches at 'Lone Pine'.

and realism. The Beveridge paddocks are needed for outdoor locations and to house a studio and production village.

It's a different approach to making a film. Almost invariably, locations are far removed from studios. Cast and crews spend days or weeks in one spot shooting exterior scenes, and inclement or inappropriate weather can cause hugely expensive delays. Interior sequences are generally shot in a city studio.

The aim at Beveridge is to bring the studio to the location. Interior and exterior sequences can be shot on the same day. If the weather is not right for an exterior shot, it's only a minor logistical problem to shoot an interior scene instead.

A simple concept, yet rarely tried anywhere before. It is to prove a godsend in the making of *ANZACS*.

The incomparable Les Binns has a key part in seeing that Beveridge works. He's a gruff, down-to-earth fellow with an almost-walrush moustache and the expression of a man with much on his mind. He generally has. As one of the most gifted and experienced art directors around (*Eureka Stockade* and *The Man from Snowy River*), he's in great demand. His central skill is his artist's eye. He trained at art school and worked his way up through the theatre, with stints at Crawford, leavened by periods travelling the country with a pop band.

The priority at Beveridge is 'to get stuck into the trenches', as Binns puts it, a task he approaches with some zeal.

The 'normal' trenches – that is, the zig-zagged holes in the ground – do not present much of a problem, especially since the Starbucks also own an earth-moving and plant-hire firm in Melbourne. David Starbuck senior has arranged, as

The 'above-ground trench', used here for a scene at Lone Pine. The cramped conditions allow little room for camera placement.

The 'above-ground trench' proves equally suitable for a night scene filmed with arc lights in the Beveridge studio.

part of the deal, that his equipment be used for the excavations. Several kilometres of trenches are gouged from the hillsides and other areas are churned into a sea of muck and mud reminiscent of the Somme and Flanders.

As the old soldiers knew only too well, 'the trenches were hell'. Holes in the ground, exposed to the ill temper of a wet and extended winter, could also present problems for cast and crews. Binns thinks long about it and comes up with the trench for all seasons. Basically, it is made up of sections of polystyrene and hessian. Each piece can be moved and used indoors or out, and pieces can be joined to make whichever trench interior is required. The walls and joins are then smeared with mud. Add a few corpses, some general debris and perhaps some logs (as at Lone Pine) and presto: the genuine, all-purpose ANZAC trench.

There will be many dirty days at Beveridge when cast and crew will bless Binns' ingenuity.

The next problem is how to simulate several French villages, intact or in ruins, and the contrasting Australian country town.

The solution is to build a composite set with an adaptable basic construction. The edifice rises in the middle of an open paddock at Beveridge. From the road, it is one of the wierdest looking structures imaginable. It's a mass of haphazard lines, exposed timbers and plyboard, held upright by rows of angled stays. It's like a derelict's dream-house, fashioned from the pickings of a council tip.

But seen from within, it's magic.

Here is an authentic French village, with rustic buildings of one and two storeys, peaked slate roofs, shuttered windows. There are gabled cottages; there are the *boulangerie*, the *estaminet*, stables, the mullioned fronts of tiny shops. It's a stunning replica of provincial France at the beginning of the century. To achieve the effect, Binns

A break in filming during a scene at the wrecked village

and his co-designers have used archival material and specially commissioned photographs of the Somme area, where buildings of the First World War period still stand. Researcher Fay Johnson has come up with diary entries of old soldiers reflecting their impressions of buildings and village life.

With adroit alterations, such as covering the slate roofs with iron, selectively retouching the front and adding the obligatory outback verandah, the set can be transformed into an equally authentic Australian country town. It's possible to film a French scene at one end of the village and an Australian scene at the other. Finally, the war-torn French village is to be wrecked, with machines puncturing holes in the roofs and walls, the facades daubed with black paint, the streets strewn with rubble.

In one form or another, the village is to feature in more than fifty scenes of *ANZACS*.

The production crews also have to be housed at the Beveridge site. Again, the sets are multifunctional. A series of weatherboard huts – doubling as a Great War army barracks – houses the production offices – design, wardrobe, make-up, even a caravan-sized mobile loo.

The studio has to be big enough to house a multitude of sets, cope with the substantial paraphernalia of lights and equipment and accommodate fifty or more people at a time. It's clear from the start that this is going to be a major expense.

Les Binns comes up with a great find. During a trip to Bendigo, he discovers a prefabricated steel factory-cum-shed for sale. It's designed to be pieced together into a structure thirty-four metres by fifty-four metres and eight metres high – as big as an aircraft hangar.

Bill Regan goes to see it and is over the moon. It's the perfect solution to the studio problem, and the price, $48 000, is a snip compared with a custom-made building. He extols the glories of the find to Burrowes and recommends that they buy it immediately.

Burrowes is less than enthusiastic.

One of the difficulties of filming a multimillion-dollar epic is that millions have to be raised through investors, both individual and corporate, via a maze of negotiations and documentation. It's a harrowing, drawn-out business that is the producer's prerogative and principal burden. To be a producer, it's essential to have the gall of the Goths. It helps if you've also got rocks in the head.

Burrowes's problem is that he hasn't got his money. There have been serious hold-ups in investment funds, Kerry Packer's funds have long gone and several hundreds of thousands of Burrowes's own cash – almost everything he's earned from *Snowy* – have been sunk into the development of *ANZACS*. With the hold-up in investment funding, the project is in crisis. Burrowes is facing ruin.

'We've got to buy it, Geoff,' Regan says.

'We're broke, mate,' Burrowes replies. 'It will have to wait until the investment is sorted out.'

'It'll be too late,' Regan insists. 'We'll never find anything better.'

Burrowes confers with Associate Producer Dennis Wright, who also says 'No'. But Regan won't give up. He keeps insisting. Somehow – nobody quite remembers the exact circumstances – a cheque is signed and the shed is bought. There's no money to transport it to Beveridge. The pieces just sit where they are.

All good crises come to an end one way or another. When *ANZACS'* money problems are happily sorted out, by which time the filming schedule has been put back almost six months, the shed is uplifted from Bendigo and erected over bare earth at Beveridge. The walls are lined with bales of hay to help with the acoustics, the sets are established, shell-holes are dug in the earth for night battleground scenes, and Les Binns's above-ground trench sections are jigsawed into myriad configurations.

The shed they couldn't afford works like a dream and saves a fortune.

While the Beveridge 'battleground' is being prepared, Wardrobe Designer Jane Hyland and Military Dresser Phil Chambers are preparing to outfit the army. A big job. The majority of scenes are set in the front lines of the Dardanelles or the Western Front. Some battle scenes – notably Amiens of 1918 – call for a cast of 300 soldiers.

Jane Hyland (*Squizzy Taylor* and *The Last Outlaw*) is used to outfitting large casts in appropriate period style, but *ANZACS* calls for something of a supreme effort. It's made clear from the outset by both Burrowes and Dixon that near enough won't be good enough. Dixon in particular is almost fanatical in his insistence that the Diggers be portrayed completely authentically. His motto is: 'If we're going to do it, let's get it absolutely right.'

The first requirement is to find 150 Anzac uniforms. The theatrical costumiers don't stock them, nor does anybody else. The uniforms will have to be made. From what material?

An exhaustive hunt round the suppliers shows that no suitable standard-issue cloth is available. The texture, the colours, the density are not right. The answer: have the cloth specially dyed and loomed. Four hundred and twenty metres are produced and 150 First World War uniforms replicated, 'button pefect'.

Phil Chambers, whose background is in props and the art department rather than costuming, has the job of seeing that the minutiae of military life are meticulously observed. Are the battalion colours right? Are the service and campaign stripes appropriate, not just to the period but to the character's history in the series? Has he been wounded in previous scenes, and, if so, does the sleeve carry appropriate wound stripes?

ANZACS covers such a span and so many harrowing battle scenes that twelve of the major characters each have four uniforms in progressive stages of dilapidation. This is how Chambers describes them: Uniform 1: 'neat, clean and new'; Uniform 2: 'well worn'; Uniform 3: 'trench-fevered'; Uniform 4: 'absolutely stuffed'.

Some of the uniforms – principally those of the British High Command – are hired. The London theatrical costumiers Bermans and Nathans supply the dress for Field Marshal Haig and other senior generals on his staff.

But Australia's senior commander, Lieutenant General Sir John Monash, gets special privileges – an outfit specially made. Bill Kerr, who plays Monash, tries it on for Director John Dixon's appraisal.

'Looks great, Bill,' says Miller, 'but it's a bit on the new side. Wear it in.'

There's nothing an actor revels in more than dressing up and 'getting into the part'. Kerr cuts a magnificent figure strutting around the shell-holes at Beveridge, drawing involuntary salutes from fellow cast members dressed as lowlier mortals. That night Kerr takes the outfit back to the hotel and sleeps in it. The morning comes, and he strides from his room to the lift, which is occupied by a party of Japanese tourists.

The effect is sensational. Burrowes recounts the story and swears that at that moment, Japan, for the second time in forty years, capitulated totally.

The soldiers are in good shape. Now they have to have weapons to fight with. Armourer Mike Warwick and Quartermaster Mike Clark, a lieutentant colonel in Vietnam, undertake this project. More than 400 weapons are needed, ranging from standard rifles to machine-guns and mortars.

The Australian .303 rifles are not hard to come by. It says something about the durability of this remarkable weapon that the Army is able to provide 300, all in good working condition – no trouble at all.

The automatic firearms pose the difficulty. The London firm of Bapty and Co. can supply the key weapons – Lewis guns, German Maxim machine-guns and Vickers guns, along with sundry firearms, including Luger and Webley revolvers, German Mausers and American

TOP: *The shoulder patch is the red and white ('blood and bandages') of the 8th Battalion. The 'A' indicates a Gallipoli veteran; the single stripe is that of a lance corporal.*

BOTTOM: *Attention to detail is essential if ANZAC soldiers are to be portrayed realistically. The armband indicated 'stretcher bearer'.*

RIGHT: *Every uniform has to carry the appropriate service colours. This is a corner of the wardrobe department.*

Springfield rifles. But Victorian State law strictly prohibits automatic weapons in private hands, and *ANZACS* requires an arsenal of such weapons.

Long and tedious negotiations with the State Government, carried out in consultation with the Victoria Police, result eventually in an order signed by the Governor in Council granting a special permit.

The armoury is finally established at Beveridge, complete with sophisticated security devices and a twenty-four-hour guard. None of the firearms has been rendered innocuous. Although only blanks are used during filming, every weapon is capable of firing live ammunition.

It's a legal, but lethal, cache, which happily survives the 'shoot' without mishap.

Casting for *ANZACS* is a huge task. There are almost 200 roles. The Australian Army – which provides substantial assistance in making the series – also contributes regular soldiers as extras. The central roles have to be filled through exhaustive auditioning.

Crawfords feature prominently in the actors' résumés. Andrew Clarke (Martin Barrington) has an impressive stage background but achieved a high profile at Crawfords (*Cop Shop, The Sullivans, Special Squad*); Megan Williams (Kate) appeared in *The Sullivans;* Jonathan Sweet (Bill the Pom) appeared in *Carson's Law* and *Special Squad*; Jon Blake (Flanagan) has a varied background and also starred in *Special Squad.* There are old stagers like Tony Bonner (Harold Armstrong), who has appeared in just about everything since and including *Skippy.* Bill Kerr (Monash) has a distinguished background that goes back even further – to BBC radio and the West End – and includes Australian television and feature films.

Some of the major historical figures – Haig, Lloyd George – have to be portrayed by actors who have a strong screen presence and the authentic British bearing and accent.

Initially, Burrowes thinks that he may have to import British actors to get the parts right. Then Noel Trevarthan proves to have the exact qualities for Haig, although he is not British born but a New Zealander. He played Gerard in *Carson's Law* and has had twenty-five years in films and television in Britain.

Lloyd George, the fiery Welshman who becomes Prime Minister and a bitter opponent of Haig, seems even more difficult to cast. Dixon comes across the name Rhys McConnochie in *Showcase*, the actors' directory. On the basis that anyone named Rhys must be Welsh, McConnochie is asked to audition. He's perfect, both in his bearing and his ability to reproduce the full and fruity Taffy accent.

It's an indication of McConnochie's calibre that he carries the role so well. The surname is the clue: his background is not Welsh but Scottish.

There's a central role still not cast: that of the irreverent larrikin Pat Cleary. Cleary is Dixon's creation, a character dear to his heart and the focus of humour within a series of sombre fabric. It seems that Dixon has fashioned Cleary after one notable Australian: the comedian and television personality Paul Hogan.

The part is clearly 'made' for Hogan. The question is whether he can possibly be persuaded to take it. He has become a cult figure in Australia and Britain. The Americans are soon to pay great attention to him. He's a comedian of exceptional talent and has achieved success not simply by performing but by writing most of his own material, and largely controlling the product put to air. Historically, Hogan has never been *part* of the act. Shows have invariably been shaped around him. Also, he's never accepted a major acting role, let alone one that, in the case of *ANZACS*, could demand twenty weeks of his working life.

Undaunted, Burrowes rings John Cornell, Hogan's partner and manager, and suggests that Hogan look at the *ANZACS* scripts.

'Sure, we'll always read scripts,' Cornell responds laconically. 'But I better warn you we've knocked back the last fifty-two.'

Burrowes presses on. The scripts are parcelled and sent to Cornell in Sydney. Burrowes is convinced that Hogan and Cornell will say 'No', but he's got nothing to lose.

Several weeks later, there's a call from Cornell. 'Paul likes the scripts, mate,' says Cornell. 'Maybe we can get together and have a talk.'

Burrowes is delighted. Hogan is showing interest, and latterly there's been a dramatic rise in Hogan's fortunes. He's been featured in television commercials in the United States encouraging tourism to Australia. They have proved a sensation. One of the American networks has included a three-minute special on him in their coast-to-coast news service. It's an almost unheard-of response to an Australian performer. Hogan shows signs of extending the cult following already enjoyed in Australia and Britain to the United States. Burrowes is well aware that Hogan's name on *ANZACS* could vastly improve the series' potential international sale.

Not long after, Burrowes and Dennis Wright meet Cornell at the Hilton in Melbourne. Burrowes talks long and enthusiastically about the plans for the series. The response is good. Then Cornell drops a bombshell.

'We've got a bit of a worry. The Yanks have offered Paul a couple of network specials.'

The ultimate for any performer: coast-to-coast exposure in the world's biggest television market. A superb opportunity. An offer that clearly puts Hogan's appearance in *ANZACS* out of the question.

Burrowes, disappointed, accepts the inevitable. He begins to counsel Cornell on the pros and cons of the network offer.

Cornell interrupts:

'. . . what we've been thinking is maybe it's a bit early to do network. Maybe we should wait. We reckon Paul should do *ANZACS* instead.'

Burrowes is still talking about the network offers. He sees Cornell and Dennis Wright looking strangely at him.

The penny drops.

'You mean you're saying "Yes" to *ANZACS?*'

'That's about it, mate,' Cornell says with a grin.

Burrowes takes it in, then says:

'Well, bugger me dead!'

So *ANZACS,* complete with Hogan, is underway. The addition of a star with such potential drawing power has encouraged Burrowes to enlarge the scope of the series. He seeks more money from his investors, and the budget rises from $6.5 million to $8 million. Hogan's fee is not the prime reason. As Burrowes recounts it, Cornell has been anxious not to stunt the project by making excessive demands for the star. Consequently, the figure agreed proves a happy compromise. The additional funds are largely to add greater polish, so that *ANZACS*' overseas sales potential is enhanced.

A bigger budget means a better opportunity to portray the aphorism 'War is hell'. Cast and crew get the message quickly. It's the dog-end of winter, and at Beveridge the conditions are absolutely foul.

The rain falls incessantly, the wind howls and the ground becomes a bog. Binns's above-ground trenches are blessed as priceless possessions, and the studio shed is a haven, where, even though it's freezing, scenes can be filmed safe from the deluge.

But this is a series where the holy grail is realism. The old soldiers fought and died in conditions like this. The cast and crew have to fight in them too – and suffer.

Early on in the shoot, Beveridge is renamed 'Pleurisy Plains'.

In the trenches and in 'no-man's-land', there's a sea of mud. Pumps are brought in to reduce the water levels. Everybody wears gumboots. Everybody *stops* wearing gumboots. They've either been lost in the mud or discarded in favour of laced footwear that stays on in the mire.

Paul Hogan arrives, bronzed and dapper after receiving the full star treatment in the United

ABOVE: *Paul Hogan (Pat Cleary) on the set with some of Cleary's souvenirs.*

OPPOSITE: *The battleground at Beveridge is a swamp. Strawb (Stephen Scully) takes a 'swim' in a shell-hole.*

Director of Photography Keith Wagstaff and Lighting Cameraman John Haddy try on German helmets during a break in filming at Beveridge.

States. He's been lavished with luxury and has seduced millions with his commercials, which show him swanning it in a swimming pool, extolling a sunburnt Australia.

He gets his comeuppance when, as Pat Cleary, he's dumped in a trench filled with slops.

There's one day that Director of Photography Keith Wagstaff says he – and everybody else associated with it – will never forget. Conditions are abominable. The rain falls in sheets, the wind is cyclonic, the temperature arctic. Wagstaff has learnt a lot about filming in inhospitable circumstances. In the Australian Alps, where he was Director of Photography for *The Man from Snowy River*, he discovered the value of the 'spinning glass' – a transparent disc that rotates at speed in front of the camera, keeping even the most violently driven rain off the lens.

The disc allows filming to continue on this day. But it means that cast and crew are brought almost to the end of their tether. Everyone is aching with the cold and drenched by the incessant rain. Some are literally ill. Director George Miller, who triumphed over the alpine conditions when shooting *Snowy* and survived sub-zero temperatures on a more recent film in Yugoslavia, is almost felled by 'Pleurisy Plains'. He wraps blankets around his waist to restore circulation and huddles in a makeshift shelter, vowing that his next film will be animated.

Burrowes and Dixon pick up a *Croix de Guerre*. They do not have to suffer the execrable conditions. But they express loyalty to the 'troops' by spending the day shivering along with everybody else. This demonstration of valour is noted, and appreciated.

The particularly foul conditions lead to the emergence at Beveridge of a new breed – the Mad Monks. On inclement days they appear in the vicinity of the cameras, heads shrouded, bodies

TOP: *Writer and creator of* ANZACS, *John Dixon puts on his director's hat at Beveridge.* BOTTOM: *Director George Miller in consultation with cast and crew at Beveridge.*

draped to the ankles in strange garb. It's Wagstaff, Lighting Cameraman John Haddy and entourage. They have discovered 'Driza-Bone' – an awful-looking oilskin garment long recognized as 'the farmer's friend'. It keeps them 'dry as a bone', but it also endows them with the appearance of some strange religious sect, treading the mire with sinister intent.

It's not all 'hell' out there. There are good days, too. When the sun shines, the air is balmy. Yet, wet or dry, the production manages to proceed on schedule. *ANZACS* is something of an oddity in its logistics and the manner of filming. There are five two-hour episodes, two filming units and three directors. No director is fully responsible for any single episode but rather controls individual scenes. One unit will work with Miller, another with Dixon or Pino Amenta, who learnt his craft at Crawfords. Scenes shot by all three directors are married to make each episode.

It's a method many film makers would consider untenable and a sure recipe for disaster. Not so with *ANZACS*. It's efficient, and it works.

One impediment on the road to triumph is the tank – the *sine qua non* of any good Western Front story. At least one fully mobile model is essential for *ANZACS*. There are Second World War tanks around, but none from the Great War. A replica has to be built.

The job goes to the Melbourne firm of Able Sheet Metal Industries, whose managing director, Charles Spiteri, is much admired for his ingenuity with things metal and mechanical. Spiteri, a veteran car enthusiast, and his staff obtain an old D-4 caterpillar-track bulldozer chassis. It is stripped back to the basic shell, leaving only the frame, engine and drive shaft. A heavy-duty frame is fitted to house the new superstructure, made entirely of steel. The mas-

The main ANZACS' *cast pose at ease by a field ambulance at Beveridge.*

LEFT: *The tanks that don't move. This one will take part in a battle scene. From one angle, it looks like the real thing . . . but viewed from elsewhere, the illusion is spoilt.*

RIGHT: *Make-up Supervisor Fiona Campbell assists the 'injured' during the filming of a scene in France.*

sive tracks of the Mark V are replicated by extending the drive shafts and elongating the original D-4 tracks by adding track sections from five other bulldozers.

This is wizard stuff–a mechanical sleight of hand that sounds simple but is extremely complicated and time-consuming. The budget is $35 000, a large sum for a mechanical prop. But the materials and the time spent devising it show that it has become a labour of love for Spiteri, definitely not a profitable exercise.

The tank looks magnificent. It's a monster, eight metres long, two and a half metres high and three and a half metres wide. It represents the Mark V to a T.

It arrives at 'Pleurisy Plains' amid great excitement and expectation–the biggest mobile prop ever built for an Australian film. But, as the old soldiers discovered at Bullecourt in 1917, tanks did not always live up to their reputation.

The *ANZAC* tank baulks when started. The auxiliary motor that fires the diesel engine is temperamental. The elderly D-4 clutch seizes up. The driver, Ron Rixon, almost chokes on diesel fumes disgorged by the ancient engine as he perches in the bowels of this cantankerous machine.

The mortifying moment comes one day when the tank thunders along a hill. The cameras whirr. At a crucial moment, the massive superstructure throws too much weight onto one side. A track falls off.

'We were dealing with a new concept and ancient, basic equipment,' Spiteri says. 'The film crew didn't always appreciate the engineering problems involved.'

Despite the traumas, the tank finally triumphs. It looks splendid; it brings the First World War to life.

The Battle of Beveridge is almost over. There's more filming nearby at Darraweit, where a wooded area becomes the location for the Nieppe Forest; an historic stately home at Werribee, west of Melbourne, provides venues for the High Command; at Phillip Island, 120 kilometres south of Melbourne, the Gallipoli landing is impressively re-created.

By December 1984, all rushes are in the hands of Film Editor Phil Reid and other post-production staff. Bruce Rowland builds in his music.

Post-production is rarely mentioned in stories about film-making, which is a pity. For this is where much magic takes place.

ANZACS emerges as the biggest mini-series ever undertaken for Australian television. With a budget of $8 million, it is the most expensive.

Few stories have been realized with such passionate commitment to an idea or with such care for the values of Australians who lived out a great drama long ago.

Director Pino Amenta (in blue) discusses a scene with cast members during a windswept day at 'Gallipoli' – Phillip Island.

TOP: Attractive Imogen Mai (Tracey Callender) has the attention of Martin (Andrew Clarke) at a formal dinner party at the Barrington homestead, Hereford Downs, on the night war is declared. BOTTOM LEFT: *A 'sort of brotherhood' exists between Martin (Andrew Clarke) and Dick Baker (Mark Hembrow), right, who have been friends since boyhood at Hereford Downs.* BOTTOM RIGHT: *Friends since childhood, Martin (Andrew Clarke) and Kate (Megan Williams) in a carefree moment before Martin's enlistment.*

THE EPISODE OUTLINES

EPISODE 1

Victoria, Australia, July 1914

IT IS MORNING AT HEREFORD DOWNS, A beautiful, sprawling property in Victoria's Western District. Martin Barrington, the scion of a wealthy farming family, is breaking in a thoroughbred, a job he does well.

Martin has just quit university for the countryman's life he loves. He meets Dick Baker, a lifelong friend employed by the Barringtons. Dick is lively and adventurous. There's almost a brotherhood between him and Martin. The boys plan to go to Queensland to work on another property owned by the Barringtons. Martin's father, Sir Rupert Barrington, an ex-British Army officer and something of an aristocrat, has other ideas. He wants Martin to continue the family tradition and go to Cambridge. Sir Rupert is concerned about the 'summer storm' gathering in Europe and the possibility that Britain could soon be at war. If this happens, it is Australia's duty to go to the aid of the mother country. Martin, unwilling to be forced into his father's mould, is unimpressed by events half a world away. 'What's it got to do with us,' he says.

There's an arrival at Tallangarook Station: Kate Baker, Dick's sister, is back from the city after completing nursing training. Kate has a lot of character, and a sharp tongue. When her mother, Ma Baker, tells her that Martin Barrington is home, she is interested. She likes Martin, yet she sees him as indulged, too used to the silver spoon.

At a dinner party at the Barrington homestead, Sir Rupert talks of the 'indescribable enthusiasm' in Australia for the Empire's impending engagement in war. The dinner is interrupted by news that Britain has finally entered the conflict. A toast is drunk, and Sir Rupert announces that he had anticipated the war by arranging a commission for Martin with his old British regiment. Martin receives the news impassively, and later goes to tell Dick that he is going ahead with their plan for Queensland. Dick responds by announcing that he has decided to join up. He urges Martin to do the same. There is a row when Martin tells Sir Rupert that he will not take the commission. He volunteers as a private. He tells Kate he wants to look after Dick.

During training at Broadmeadows Camp near Melbourne, a camaraderie develops between the two boys and other new recruits in their platoon: the laconic Pat Cleary ('middleweight champion of North Queensland, all-time top horse-breaker of the outer Barcoo and breaker of women's hearts everywhere'); the eager and innocent Roly Collins; Bill 'the Pom' Harris, an Englishman with unexplained skills as a soldier; the close Danish brothers Karl and Eric Johansen; and the intelligent, sensitive Lieutenant Armstrong, the platoon's officer. The platoon sergeant is Tom McArthur, a football star who is no hero to the recruits. Martin is drafted as a corporal.

ENLIST NOW

TOP RIGHT: *Pat Cleary (Paul Hogan), right, meets up with other recruits at a rally at Ballarat.*

BOTTOM RIGHT: *The training camp at Broadmeadows. The new recruits are licked into shape in a 'broomstick' drill.*

LEFT: *The call to patriotism as the Honourable Cyril Earnshaw (Howard Bell) addresses a recruitment rally at Ballarat.*

Martin and Dick meet Kate unexpectedly. She has joined the nursing corps. For the first time, the privileged Martin finds himself at a social disadvantage: Kate is a lieutenant, he is only a corporal.

25 April 1915

ON THE DECK OF A DARKENED DESTROYER approaching the Dardanelles, the platoon prepares for its first taste of war. Longboats take them to the shore for a landing at Anzac Cove. Turkish guns are already blazing. There is chaos. The platoon's boat lands at the wrong place, and under heavy machine-gun fire. As the troops leap into the deep water, their heavy kits drag them down. McArthur tries to gather the platoon. Martin, Dick, Roly, Pat and Bill are together. The rifle and machine-gun fire is now continuous, and there is occasional shelling. Dead and wounded litter the hillside. Karl Johansen is hit. His brother, Eric, is crying as the platoon is ordered forward. He has to leave Karl to die. As the line advances, Eric is hit, too, and so is Roly. Roly tries to save the more seriously wounded Eric, but fails.

The rest of the platoon dive for cover in dense scrub. Martin realizes that they are far short of their objective. But McArthur gives orders to dig in. He sums up: 'The home team's got everything in their favour.' The Turks have reinforcements nearby, and they hold the high ground.

In the makeshift headquarters, General Bridges, commander of the Australian forces, suggests evacuation. Everything has gone wrong. His troops are being slaughtered. Brigadier General Walker suggests that the forward troops are holding well. The ANZAC Corps commander, Lieutenant General Birdwood, advises Bridges not to underestimate his Australians. The order

An evocative moment in Australian history – the landing at Gallipoli.

comes from British High Command rejecting evacuation, demanding that the troops 'dig, dig, dig, until they are safe'.

In a roughly dug trench, Martin is concerned about the safety of Dick, who has crept into no-man's-land to rescue wounded. Martin follows him protectively and is hit in the stomach. Roly writes to Martin in hospital, giving him the news that only eleven of the platoon's original forty are left. He tells of a new recruit, Flanagan. 'You'll like him,' Roly writes.

Kate visits Martin's hospital tent, fearing the worst, but finds him almost recovered, well enough to talk of romance. Kate feels that the class gulf between them is too great. She tells him that she can organize his convalescence in Egypt. Martin is determined to get back to his platoon to 'look after Dick'. 'Who's going to look after you?' Kate replies.

In August 1915, the order comes to stage a major assault to capture the Turkish-held heights, including Lone Pine, Hill 900 and The Nek, and link with two English divisions landed at Suvla Bay. 'Bloody murder,' Brigadier General Walker protests. But the decision has been made. Martin returns to the platoon. Keith Murdoch, war correspondent and influential adviser to Prime Minister Hughes, is also at Anzac Cove, gathering information critical of the Gallipoli campaign.

In a tense moment, Dick and Martin are involved in fierce fighting.

In London, Murdoch meets the British Prime Minister, Lloyd George, and gives him information that will result in the order to evacuate Gallipoli.

ABOVE AND OPPOSITE BOTTOM LEFT: *Up the cliff-face at Gallipoli.*

OPPOSITE TOP: *Martin (Andrew Clarke) and Dick (Mark Hembrow) consider the next move during a moment of decision at Gallipoli.*

OPPOSITE BOTTOM RIGHT: *Confrontation at Lone Pine. Dick (Mark Hembrow) enters a fortified Turkish trench.*

The brilliant Colonel White devises a plan to withdraw the 40 000 Anzacs by clever deception. A cricket match is played in sight of the Turks, night fires are lit, and 'ghost guns' are rigged. The Anzacs file away in the darkness. There is the feeling that they are betraying their dead mates by leaving. 'Australians don't bloody quit!' Pat declares angrily.

Martin pauses by Dick's grave and is persuaded by Flanagan to come away. 'If you thought about all the good ones gone, you'd go crazy,' he tells Martin. 'It was a stuff-up from the start.'

RIGHT: *The night fires burn as Gallipoli is evacuated.*

BELOW TOP: *A cricket match is staged to divert the Turks' attention from the impending evacuation of Gallipoli. McArthur (Patrick Ward) is the bowler and Roly (Christopher Cummins) the batsman. The distinctive umpire with two hats is Pat Cleary (Paul Hogan).*

BOTTOM: *Filing past the graves of fallen comrades during the evacuation of Gallipoli.*

EPISODE 2

April 1916

THE PLATOON TRAVELS IN A RAILWAY cattle truck through the tranquil French countryside. Only six of the platoon's forty 'originals' are left. Most are replacements for those lost at Gallipoli. Roly Collins introduces himself to Wilhelm Schmidt, a Wimmera wheat farmer. Flanagan defends Schmidt when the crude Dingo Gordon calls him a 'Hun'. Flanagan points out that Schmidt is 'fair dinkum'. As a mark of acceptance, he gives him the nickname 'Kaiser'.

Other reinforcements include the fresh-faced Charlie Upton, who reminds Martin of Dick Baker. Pudden Parsons, large in frame, low in IQ, and Bluey, the Lewis gunner. After Gallipoli, the boys see rural France as a paradise.

They change their minds when they reach the battlefields around Armentieres, a shell-shattered wasteland. 'I played football on a ground like this once,' says Pat in wonder.

Each in his own way adapts to the challenge of the new front line, which is considered a 'nursery' or rest sector. Pat ingeniously manages to pirate crates of Haig's whisky from a consignment bound for British headquarters. He has arranged to split the profits with the doughty, businesslike Madame of the local *estaminet*. Roly is smitten with Madame's comely daughter, Marie, but Marie only has eyes for the arch-rogue Pat.

The platoon is introduced to the harsh realities of the Western Front and ordered to carry out a trench raid. Armstrong, Martin, Flanagan and McArthur prepare to go over the top during a protective barrage. The platoon leader, Armstrong, is knocked unconscious. McArthur, who, as sergeant, is next in command, loses his nerve and stays in the trench. Martin assumes the

A new form of warfare. The Anzacs crowd a Pozieres communication trench at the Western Front.

leadership, and the platoon carries out an exceptionally successful raid on the German line. No mention is made of McArthur funking it. He gets the credit and is awarded the Military Medal.

At Chateau Beaurepaire, General (later Field Marshal) Haig, commander of the British Armies in France, discusses with his chief of staff, Lieutenant General Kiggell, reports of disorder and a 'ragamuffin mentality' among Australian troops. Haig favours the death penalty as a disciplinary measure. The Australians need blooding, he says. The Somme would be ideal.

At a smart village restaurant, Martin meets Kate again. He speaks French fluently and tries to impress her with his knowledge of wine, but finds himself at a disadvantage. He is the only one there not an officer. Kate, the lieutenant, is amused at seeing Martin put down and notes his jealousy when the other officers pay attention to her.

Keith Murdoch is received by Haig. Murdoch raises the question of the desirability of uniting all Australian divisions into one corps. Haig rejects the suggestion. He tells Murdoch that the wastage at the Western Front is 5000 a day. He hopes to end the deadlock by pitting twenty divisions against the German line – his greatest blow of the war.

Members of the platoon are depressed when orders come through for them to move out of the 'nursery' area to the Somme. At the *estaminet*, the boys encourage Pat to consummate the embryonic love affair with Marie but arrange for Madame to catch him out. The joke is on Pat, but the outcome surprises everyone.

The platoon sets off for what they have been told is 'the great battle that is going to win the war!' Roly writes of it as 'our last day of innocence'.

They take their positions in the comunication trenches at Pozieres – the scene of the heaviest artillery barrages of the war. As the guns thunder, the landscape is torn apart. Men fall or are dug out, crying, wounded, dead. Armstrong is so

TOP: *Haig (Noel Trevarthan) confers with his Chief of Staff Lieutenant General Kiggell (Michael Adams) at British Headquarters in France.*

BOTTOM: *An embarrassed Corporal Barrington (Andrew Clarke) takes Lieutenant Kate Baker (Megan Williams) to a French restaurant only to be outmanoeuvred by an unwelcome Flanagan (Jon Blake), second left, and Pat Cleary (Paul Hogan), right.*

OPPOSITE: *The platoon marches confidently through a French village on the way to the Somme.*

P GUIMOTT
CHAMBR ES POUR VOYAGEURS
H MOLLIER
BOULANGERIE

Roly's mother, Mrs Collins (Diana Greentree)—facing left—and Ma Baker (Sheila Kenneally) meet at a Comforts Fund rally in Victoria.

shaken that he cannot make decisions. Martin takes over. Each explosion plays havoc with the men's nerves. Roly has to be dug out and then snaps. Pat grabs him and holds him like a child.

In Melbourne, newspapers carry stories of great British victories along the Somme. The Honourable Cyril Earnshaw, MHR, encourages his shy librarian son, Max, to join up before it is too late and the war is over. The politician sees his own glory in his son's enlistment.

At Pozieres the British barrage is incompetently directed, shellfire completely missing the target. Within this chaos, Armstrong manages to give effective orders, which the platoon, largely at Martin's initiative, carry out with skill and courage. A German machine-gun post is taken and vital high ground gained. Total exhaustion overwhelms every member of the platoon. They collapse in a trench and fall asleep as they are—sitting, lying, standing.

Keith Murdoch has another meeting with Haig. Haig tells Murdoch that the Australian division is the only one to gain all its objectives. Murdoch is taken aback when he hears that the Germans are concentrating all their reserves on these areas to regain them. Haig admits that casualties will be enormous. He declares his policy: to engage the enemy and wear him down, shell by shell and man by man. 'It will be the side with the greatest fortitude, regardless of losses, who will force the decision,' he says.

At a Melbourne railway station, Earnshaw is declaiming the glories of the Somme to journalists while farewelling his son. Earnshaw urges others to join up. 'The battle of the Somme will

ABOVE: *The Honourable Cyril Earnshaw (Howard Bell) and Mrs Earnshaw (Valma Pratt) farewell their son Max (David Lynch) before he leaves for the war.*

LEFT: *Lady Barrington (Ilona Rodgers) and Sir Rupert Barrington (Vincent Ball) at the family home, Hereford Downs.*

BELOW: *Death, desolation and despair during the height of battle.*

mark the beginning of the triumphal march to Berlin,' he says.

The platoon is marching through a ruined village. They stagger like scarecrows, shattered, shell-shocked, manifestly aged. Onlookers, including nurses, one of them Kate Baker, gather around a sign that says, 'Well done the old 8th'. They begin to sing 'Pack up your troubles', but the voices trail away when they see the men's faces, ravaged by a battle in which Australians fell more thickly than at any other place in the Great War.

Martin is told he has won the Distinguished Conduct Medal, second only to the Victoria Cross. He laughs hysterically at the madness of war. He later writes to the Reverend Lonsdale at Tallangarook: 'We've just come from a place so terrible that even a raving lunatic could never imagine the horrors.' He questions the quality of British generals and the price paid in human life for so little gain.

But Martin has survived, and he has been reunited with Kate. At a concert, a free-for-all develops. Kate and Martin put their arms round each other, happy to be together.

Martin (Andrew Clarke) reads the official notification that he's to receive the DCM for his bravery at Pozieres. Flanagan (Jon Blake), left, looks on.

EPISODE 3

Section of the Somme battlefield, winter 1916-17

FLANAGAN, ON SENTRY DUTY, LOOKS OUT to the moonscape that is now the Somme battlefield. The winter has forced both armies to a standstill. Martin, Pat, Pudden and Dingo huddle around a miserable brazier in a trench, deep in mud. The six months at the Front have left them haggard and near exhaustion. Roly returns from patrol, thankful to be with his mates. He tells Martin how he hates the war – the lice, the mud, the cold, the death. Yet he is ambivalent. He has found happiness with his mates. 'I love the war,' he says, 'and that's got to be wrong, hasn't it, Marty?'

Second Lieutenant Max Earnshaw, fresh from training school, joins the platoon. He's taken aback by the casual discipline. 'You don't salute?' he asks Martin. 'Don't see the point,' Martin replies. The green Earnshaw orders the adjoining German trenches to be shelled, breaking the unofficial truce the platoon has made with the enemy. The senior officer makes Earnshaw sharply aware of the realities of life in the trenches. There's an unexpected development,

The freezing cold of the Somme winter. Dingo (Jim Holt), right, and Kaiser (Shane Briant) shiver in the trenches.

Pudden's (Alec Wilson) birthday. Pat has arranged every 'comfort' for him at an officer-only blue-light brothel.

discovered soon after: the Germans have evacuated the forward trenches and withdrawn to the Hindenburg Line.

On leave out of the line, Pat, Pudden and Flanagan look for ways to celebrate Pudden's birthday. Pat, with his ample bankroll, buys entry into an officers-only blue-light brothel. They are rudely interrupted by British MPs looking for them. The quick-thinking Flanagan outmanoeuvres them.

The platoon moves to the Hindenburg Line, an impregnable fortress of concrete and barbed wire, where the Germans have established a formidable defence.

Told that the Australians have been ordered to attack and break the line at Bullecourt, Bill the Pom observes, 'It's Pozieres all over again!' When the attack is made, the Australian Brigadier General 'Pompey' Elliott decides to withdraw his section of the Fourth Division. Martin is furious at British commander General Gough's incompetence. The new wonder weapon – the tank – which was to be the key to the attack, has failed miserably.

The platoon members go into no-man's-land to retrieve Fourth Division casualties. McArthur is mortally wounded but refuses Flanagan's efforts to drag him to safety. In the hail of shell and machine-gun fire, Pudden loses control and deserts to no-man's-land. Armstrong is showing signs of cracking up.

TOP: *The storming of the pill-box at Broodseinde Ridge. Flanagan (Jon Blake) makes his run under a hail of fire.*
BOTTOM: *The pill-box is reached. Grenades will be used to put it out of action.*

Unexpectedly, the platoon hears it is to get Blighty leave and that Martin has been commissioned in the field. Flanagan is promoted to corporal, Kaiser Schmidt is awarded the Military Medal and becomes a lance corporal. Armstrong is made a captain, in charge of the company.

There is a rumour that Pudden is with a group of deserters on the old battlefield. Armstrong orders Flanagan to find Pudden and bring him back so that he can be classified AWOL rather than as a deserter liable to a life sentence. Martin joins Flanagan. They face danger when they confront the deserters but persuade the ringleader, 'Major' Edward Kelly, to allow Pudden to return with them.

On the way through France, Martin, in his lieutenant's uniform, meets Kate. 'You're a gentleman by act of parliament,' she observes wryly. She adds the news that she also is going to England for further training.

In London, Martin has a meeting with Keith Murdoch and complains about the overuse of Australian troops and the incompetence of elements of the British leadership. Murdoch talks to Lloyd George, who reveals Haig's plans for yet another big offensive–this time at Ypres. Murdoch hears of mutinies in sixty-one French divisions. Lloyd George speaks of his determination to curb 'The Butcher' by demanding success at each stage: otherwise men and supplies will be withheld from the Western Front.

Martin and Kate are an elegant couple at a grand ball at Mayfair House in London. Martin arranges for them to be announced as 'Lieutenant and Mrs Barrington from Australia'. When Kate reacts, Martin says to her, 'I wanted you to hear what it sounded like.'

When members of the platoon board the train to return to France, Kate is there to farewell Martin. She says 'I love you', but the words are drowned out by the screech of the train's whistle.

At the British headquarters in France, Haig tells his generals he intends to direct the greatest blow in history at the Germans by using thirty divisions supported by the largest array of weaponry ever assembled. He plans to bleed the enemy white and is prepared for 300 000 British casualties in achieving this.

In Flanders, two months into the Ypres campaign, spirits are raised after Anzac victories in the battle of Menin Road. Haig writes to Lloyd George to tell him of the success and that he intends to thrust foward towards the ridge at Passchendaele.

The platoon, which Pudden has rejoined after being punished for being AWOL, is serving in the Ypres area. Captain Armstrong is diagnosed as unfit for action. 'I'm coming apart at the seams, Martin,' he says. He takes Martin's hand in a moment of emotion.

Armstrong's replacement, Captain Young, is a disaster. His priority is discipline. Martin man-

Pudden is unceremoniously returned by British MPs after undergoing detention for being AWOL.

TOP: *Troops huddle in a shell-hole during the abortive Battle of Bullecourt.*

MIDDLE: *Dingo (Jim Holt) turns in fury on a captured German after Martin is shot.*

BOTTOM: *Cleary (Paul Hogan) pays scant respect to the newly arrived Captain Young (Edmund Pegge).*

RIGHT: *Comrades fall as Flanagan (Jon Blake) leads the charge on an enemy machine-gun post.*

ages a meeting with Kate at a hospital close to the line. They make love in an available room. Martin talks about their future at Hereford Downs. There's a sense of foreboding in Kate's response.

The platoon is engaged in the assault on Broodseinde at the approach to Passchendaele. The new Captain Young's incompetence endangers his men. Flanagan knocks him unconscious, and Martin takes over. With their complete understanding of each other, the platoon takes a German blockhouse. German prisoners emerge. In an upper storey of the blockhouse, a machine-gun swivels. Shots are fired, and Martin falls. In an ugly incident, the Australians, led by Dingo, bayonet the helpless prisoners. Max Earnshaw stops them, but then he is blinded by shellfire.

Heavy rain begins to fall ominously on the Ypres battleground.

Kate goes to the field hospital, where Martin lies motionless, moaning with pain. She begs the doctor not to give him morphine, which will make him sleep and perhaps lose his hold on life. Kate sits with Martin, demanding he open his eyes. She talks of their childhood together. She slaps him. Kate's fight for Martin's life continues for many hours. Then his eyes flicker. At dawn the doctor finds Kate asleep at the foot of the bed. Martin is awake, his eyes fixed on Kate.

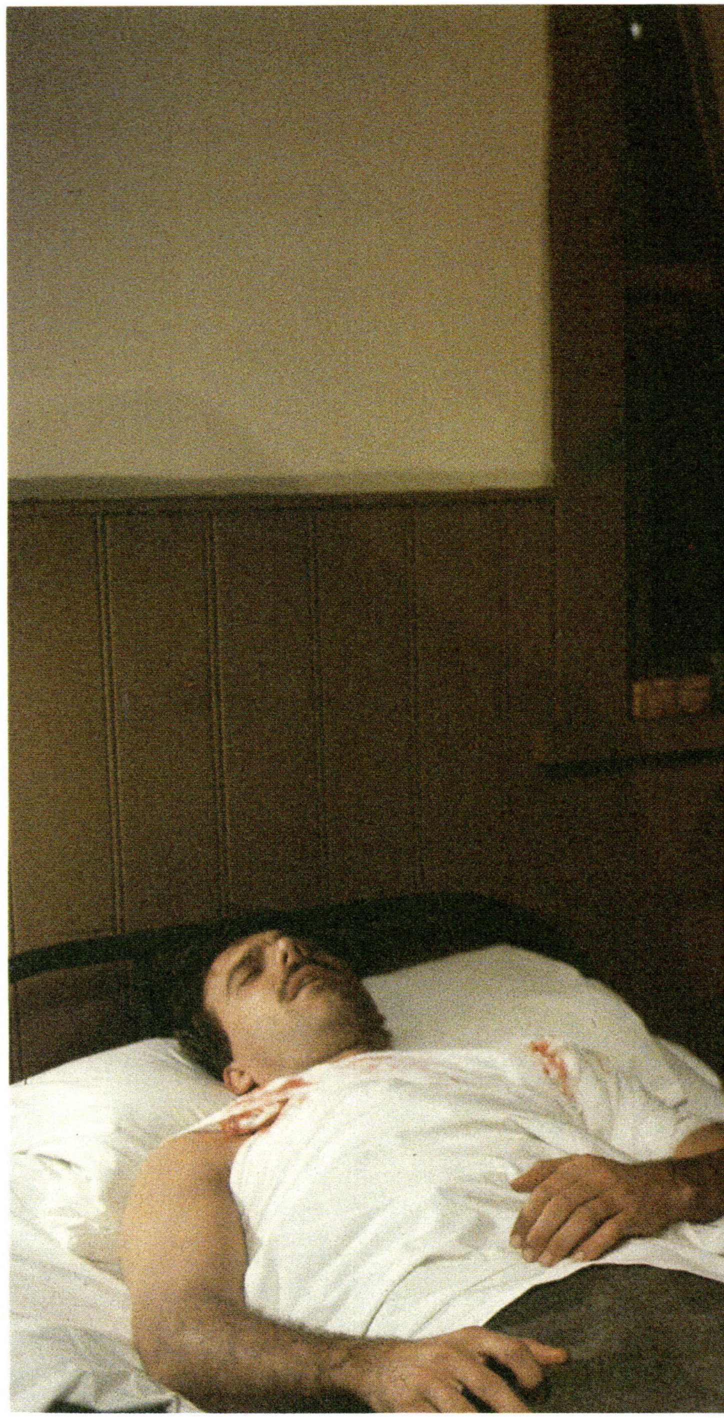

At a field hospital, Kate (Megan Williams) pleads with staff not to administer morphine to Martin and allow him to 'slip away'.

EPISODE 4

Passchendaele, Flanders 1917

THE RAIN SHEETS DOWN. THE PLATOON IS huddled in a trench, already a quagmire. Occasional shells spurt liquid mud. Relief was due ten hours ago. Flanagan wades and slithers among the men, trying to lift morale. The Canadians have taken Passchendaele, he tells them. Nobody's much impressed.

The relief party of British soldiers finally arrives, exhausted by a journey through mud that has taken eleven hours. The platoon retires across a battleground that has become a swamp. The mud is up to their waists. There are dead bodies, ditched wagons, horses up to their necks in mire.

The battlefield reflects the failed hopes of the year's offensive.

At the first road, there is a staff car with a pennant flying. Haig's Chief of Staff, General Kiggell, gets out and looks at the scene of horror. Flanagan sees he is crying. 'Oh God, did we send men to fight in this?' Kiggell says.

LEFT: *In Flanders, the trenches are turned into a quagmire . . .* BELOW: *Haig's Chief of Staff, Lieutenant General Kiggell (Michael Adams), sees the Flanders battlefields for the first time. 'My God,' he says, 'did we send men to fight in this?'*

LEFT: *Flanagan (Jon Blake) celebrates in the* estaminet *after hearing he has been commissioned as an officer.*
TOP: *The Reverend Lonsdale (Robert Coleby) and Ma Baker (Sheila Kenneally) discuss a letter from Kate refusing her mother's request to return home.*
BOTTOM: *The convalescing Martin (Andrew Clarke) receives an unexpected visit from his platoon members. Pat Cleary (Paul Hogan) copes with the matron's ire.*

Fate catches up with Flanagan over the Captain Young incident. He is dressed down in Young's presence. Then Young is asked to leave. The errors of 'green' officers are admitted. Flanagan is told he is to be commissioned as a second lieutenant.

The old friends, Roly, Pat, Bill and Flanagan, visit Martin, still bandaged but recovering in hospital. They farewell him fondly, assuming he will soon be in Australia. Kate suspects that he will not go home. 'I'll miss him like blazes,' she says, 'but I want him to go.'

At Ma Baker's cottage at Tallangarook, the Reverend Lonsdale reads a letter from Kate refusing Ma Baker's appeal for her to come home.

Kate has her own disappointment. In London, she meets the convalescing Martin, who tells her he is not returning to Australia but is seeking a staff job. It is clear that he wants to get back to his platoon. 'Go then,' Kate tells him bitterly. 'Shove off and play soldiers.'

Martin meets Murdoch at a London club and stresses the dissatisfaction with elements of the British staff. Murdoch reveals that there are already plans to unite five Australian divisions under Australian command. He tells Martin there may be a staff job with Major General Monash's Third Division.

Martin is in Amiens when the German Army, strengthened by sixty divisions released from the collapsed Russian Front, makes its great offensive in March 1918. The advance is so swift that communications have been cut and British forces are in rapid retreat.

Reporting to Monash's headquarters, Martin finds there is confusion about the extent of the German advance. He tells Monash he knows the area well. He volunteers to locate the German positions, commandeering a staff car to do so. He finds a party of English engineers, gives the car to wounded British soldiers coming out of the line, and digs in with the engineers, who are without an officer.

The staff car is driven to a field hospital, where the wounded are to be treated. Kate asks where the car came from. The soldiers show the authorization chit signed by Martin. 'I might have known,' she says.

Lloyd George tells Murdoch that the Germans have broken through on two fronts – on the Somme and in Flanders. They have taken Bullecourt, Bapaume, Albert, Pozieres. Lloyd George adds the sobering news that the Allies may lose the war. The only reserves left are five Australian divisions, the Canadians and a few battered British divisions.

Members of the original platoon are transported by train to Hazebrouck as part of the Australian First Division's attempt to stop a German thrust cutting off the vital channel ports.

Bill the Pom's secret is discovered as they march to the front line. He is recognized as a British Army regular who shot an officer and

TOP LEFT: *The British Prime Minister, Lloyd George (Rhys McConnochie), confers with General Wilson (Jon Sidney) about removing Haig.*

TOP RIGHT: *Battalion members wait in ambush for the advancing Germans in the Nieppe Forest.*

LEFT: *The secret of Bill 'the Pom' (Jonathan Sweet) is revealed during a dramatic confrontation with a British officer of the Buffs (Gareth Wilding-Forbes).*

OPPOSITE: *Martin (Andrew Clarke) reports to Major General Monash (Bill Kerr) for a new job as staff officer with divisional command.*

deserted in Afghanistan before the war. Bill fends off arrest by threatening to shoot the Buffs officer who has challenged him.

The platoon, part of the 8th Battalion, digs in near a farmhouse in the Nieppe Forest. Bill proves an expert in camouflage and concealment. Lieutenant Flanagan commands the force of ninety-seven men. Bill observes that it would take at least 600 to hold this section of the front. An ingenious form of scattered defence is organized, with grass covering the emplacements so that defence lines are not seen. The enterprising Pat discovers a cache of women's silk underwear – silk is a prized protection against lice – which platoon members put on. British soldiers, including a colonel, join the motley crew for what will become known as 'Flanagan's last stand'. The first line of advancing Germans approaches through the mist. They are mown down by the concealed guns of Flanagan's mob. In a defensive operation, superbly coordinated, British cavalry sweep in to support the defence. Flanagan requests British artillery to shell his own position to stop the advance, now almost on top of them. The attack is fought off, the position held. The Buffs officer who had threatened to arrest Bill is impressed enough to forget the past. 'I saw an Australian sergeant major in action who would have been a credit to the Buffs themselves,' he says.

The significance of the First Australian Divisions's defeat of elements of six German divisions at Nieppe was not acknowledged by the British Command.

Martin and Kate meet at a French cafe. Kate calls Martin a 'perpetual schoolboy' for wanting to be back where there is danger. 'There'll be more unprincipled men alive at the end of the war than the other kind,' she says. 'Why should my man be one of the old-fashioned kind?'

At night in a hotel bedroom, Martin wakes from a nightmare. Kate hugs him. They both know what the dream was about.

RIGHT: *Flanagan (Jon Blake) preparing for action in a night raid.*

BELOW: *British cavalry charge during 'Flanagan's last stand' in the Nieppe Forest.*

EPISODE 5

French countryside – a section post, mid-1918

THERE IS A WELCOME BREAK IN THE tempo of the war. Platoon members relax in an idyllic, unspoilt area of the French countryside. Pat and Pudden play cards. The serenity is interrupted by the arrival of a callow and remarkably clumsy new recruit, Carter. Pat seeks solace at the *estaminet*, which is jammed with American soldiers. He proceeds to make history by losing all his money in a crap game.

The platoon moves into the forward lines in farmland along the Somme. Pat decides to overcome his new-found penury by making a lone sortie into German lines. He is looking for souvenirs to sell to the Americans. He succeeds handsomely and brings back five German prisoners in the process.

At Bertangles, a French manor house, Australian senior officers gather for an address by the commander of the newly formed Australian Corps, Lieutenant General Sir John Monash. The corps is the largest in France, with 166 000 men. Monash declares that he wants to see more recognition of the Australian soldiers' achievements. He also wants them to become better acquainted with the new weapon: the tank.

Martin and Kate picnic together on a sunlit day. The war is a world away. Martin talks of his admiration for Monash, but Kate is cynical. 'Idealism has so far only filled the cemeteries,' she says. Kate gambles: she offers to resign from nursing and return to Australia if Martin will request a transfer home. Martin refuses. He feels he cannot walk out on the war or his mates. 'It won't be long, love,' he says. Kate shows anger, then fear.

Senior officers of the newly formed Australian Army Corps pose with their commander, Lieutenant General Sir John Monash.

ABOVE: *Childhood friends who went to war together and become lovers—Martin Barrington and Kate Baker (Andrew Clarke and Megan Williams).*

LEFT: *Pat Cleary (Paul Hogan) makes an unofficial foray behind the German lines and brings back prisoners, plus a welcome supply of champagne.*

Monash's plans for the significant battle of Hamel are disturbed by the threatened withdrawal, at the last moment, of 2000 American troops. The American soldiers are not happy. Pat consoles them by teaching them two-up, with satisfying results – for Pat. Roly spends his time with Madame's daughter, Marie. He suggests that when the war ends they go back to Australia together.

The Hamel battle – with American participation – is a stunning success. Martin manages to be close to his old battalion in the guise of staff observer. He is rebuked by Blamey for involving himself at the battlefront. Martin presses his constant request to be allowed to return to his old battalion.

The platoon is involved in the later stages of the Battle of Amiens, where the Canadian and Australian corps break through the German lines – 'the black day of the German Army', as the German General Ludendorff describes it.

During fighting, Flanagan takes refuge in a British tank. There's an unexpected occupant: Martin, released from staff duties, has hitched a ride to get to the battalion, which he is to rejoin as a company commander. There is a gas attack, and Roly becomes a casualty.

Troops advance en masse during the battle of Lihons.

TOP: *Flanagan (Jon Blake), centre, deals roughly with a German prisoner following the capture of a machine-gun position. The Germans have shot their own officer for refusing to surrender.*

MIDDLE: *Pudden (Alec Wilson) leaps to the attack.*

BOTTOM: *The blinding smoke and the wire claim their victims.*

RIGHT: *The biggest scene in* ANZACS. *A tank blazes and an aircraft flies low over the smoke-filled battlefield near Lihons.*

In a field hospital, Roly is visited by Kate. He tells her that the platoon has been reduced to fifteen and adds 'Martin is going great guns. You'd be proud of him,' but then realizes he may have said something wrong.

Problems are emerging within the Australian forces. Losses have resulted in the order for the 60th Battalion to be disbanded. The men refuse to obey. The much-respected Brigadier General 'Pompey' Elliott confronts them and restores order.

Kate is visited by Roly. He asks her to see Marie, who is sick. Kate diagnoses the deadly Spanish influenza.

As part of the continuing advances on the Somme, Martin leads his company across a smoke-filled battleground. It is clear that he exults in being back in the front line. Flanagan is leading the platoon from the flank. He sees Martin and others advancing towards an unseen German machine-gun post. Flanagan charges the thick wire, leaps from one strand to another and silences the German position. It is a piece of impossible bravery. Martin sends a runner back with a message recommending the Victoria Cross for Flanagan.

Flanagan (Jon Blake) leaps the wire in a dramatic attempt to save Martin. He is to be awarded the VC for this action.

It is the last days of the war. The platoon is clearing the remaining Germans from a wrecked village. There is a turning point in the story.

Soon after, Flanagan announces that the platoon is 'out of a job'. The war is over.

There is a celebration at the *estaminet*. Kate and Flanagan dance in a moment of wild revelry. Roly arrives, carrying chocolates for the sick Marie. He goes to her room and then returns, still holding the gift. Marie is dead.

On the troopship carrying the soldiers home, Roly remembers the war. He dreads the question: 'What was it like?' He feels he can never answer it. 'Us and our families will live with a four-year gap for the rest of our lives,' he says. 'It's not that Australia's changed – we have.'

At Tallangarook, the chief characters gather for the unveiling of a memorial to those fallen in the war. Wreaths are laid, and the bugler plays. The sights and sounds of war are remembered. The blue Australian sky changes to the grey of northern Europe. The grass has begun to take over the scarred battlefields. Blood-red poppies bow their heads in the gentle breeze.

Kate (Megan Williams) remembers the fallen at a graveyard near the Somme battlefields. Roly (Christopher Cummins) is with her.

THE CAST AND CREW

PAUL HOGAN – *Pat Cleary*

Paul Hogan's place in the history of Australian entertainment is secure. Though his television appearances are carefully rationed and comparatively rare, no other Australian has approached the scope of his appeal.

Admired by university dons, aped by school children, 'Hoges' has the quintessential appeal of all great comedians. Deep down we like to think there's a little bit of Hoges in us all.

Australians understood almost instantly, when Hogan, then employed as a rigger, came down from Sydney Harbour Bridge early in the 1970s, that here was a talent that owed nothing to past performers or other countries, and everything to his own time and to his country.

Since then Paul Hogan has demonstrated that his appeal goes beyond this country. He is the only Australian comic to have enjoyed success both in England and the United States. In each country, through television commercials, he is a cult figure.

And like most great comedians, Hogan has never disguised his ambition to be a dramatic actor. In *ANZACS* he realizes that ambition.

Pat Cleary comes from somewhere way out there. You name it, Bourke or the Barcoo – he's been there. A shearer, fencer, horse-beaker and roustabout, he belongs to that army of inland drifters who so wonderfully served the outback stations at the turn of the century.

He is a member of the AWU who remembers the great shearers' strike. In 1914, passing through Ballarat and seeing Martin and Dick in a recruiting march, he peels himself off a lamp post and joins in. 'Dunno what came over me,' he said later.

On the ship going over, Pat starts a two-up school that lasts the rest of the war. He also runs a book on anything the boys will bet on – and if you want anything, just ask Pat.

In France, Pat becomes the souvenir king and an expert on all items of German equipment. He also becomes a very special friend of Madame at the *estaminet*, and their relationship is mutually profitable in more than one way.

Pat has seen too much and lived too much in the bush to ever feel the need to take life seriously. He lives it for the day – but what days they are.

He is always there when the whips are cracking. Curiously, despite this, he is a survivor. He returns to the bush the way he came down, jumping the rattler, but with a wallet that has to be carried in the freight car.

Pat Cleary is the Australian larrikin – irreverent, shameless, humorous and irrepressible.

TONY BONNER – *Harold Armstrong*

A Penguin Award winner and twice winner of Sammy Awards for Best Actor, Tony Bonner is one of Australia's best-known and most accomplished actors.

In *ANZACS*, Bonner plays Harold Armstrong, a sensitive, intelligent schoolteacher. In battle he is the calm in the eye of the storm, but the psychological strains finally catch up with him at Ypres, and he is sent home with DAH (disorganized action of the heart). Many thousands were afflicted by this debilitating condition in the First World War. Though he survives, Armstrong is one of the most tragic characters in the series.

ANDREW CLARKE – *Martin Barrington*

A graduate of NIDA, Andrew Clarke's stage career was solidly founded on the modern classics. He has played Judge Breck in *Hedda Gabler* for the Adelaide Repertory, the son in *Long Day's Journey into Night*, Tom in *The Glass Menagerie* and the narrator and four other roles in *Under Milkwood*. In 1979 he took the lead role in the award-winning Edinburgh Festival production of *Errol Flynn's Great Adventure Book for Boys*.

A former Australian Rules footballer with Adelaide's Sturt Football Club, Andrew has played television detectives in *Cop Shop*, *The Sullivans* and *Special Squad*, as well as roles in *Bellamy*, *Prisoner*, *Taurus Rising* and *A Country Practice*.

In *Sara Dane* he played an English officer. In *ANZACS* he plays an Australian officer, a central character throughout the series.

Martin Barrington, DCM, is representative of the social order existing in the Australia of 1914. Born to wealth, he is very much of his class and background – Hereford Downs (the Barrington holding), Melbourne Grammar and Melbourne University.

But he defies his class by insisting on joining the army as a private, and it is not until after he wins the DCM that he is commissioned in the field. Later he is posted to Monash's staff, where he sees at first hand the drama of the German offensive and the formation of the Australian Corps.

Towards the end, he can see no life beyond the war. He is a psychological casualty long before he becomes a physical casualty.

BILL KERR – *Lieutenant General Sir John Monash*

Internationally known, Bill Kerr left Australia in 1947 and almost at once enjoyed success on radio, in the West End, in television and films. He returned to Australia three years ago to find himself in great demand for a variety of roles in films as diverse as *Dusty* and *Gallipoli*.

We first see Monash at Gallipoli. Martin Barrington becomes his protégé and is our interpreter of this complex man, who, had the war gone on, could have become the Commander-in-Chief of the British Armies in France.

ILONA RODGERS – *Lady Barrington*

Ilona Rodgers brings her extensive theatre and television experience to the role of Lady Theodora Barrington – beautiful, intelligent, outspoken and educated in Germany and Switzerland.

Lady Barrington and her son, Martin, are natural allies. In his absence, she is drawn towards her intellectual and social equal, the Anglican vicar, George Lonsdale.

Tony Bonner (Harold Armstrong)

Andrew Clarke (Martin Barrington)

Bill Kerr (Monash)

Ilona Rodgers (Lady Barrington)

Jim Holt (Dingo Gordon)

Jonathan Sweet (Bill 'the Pom')

Jon Blake (Flanagan)

Shane Briant (Kaiser)

JIM HOLT – *Dingo Gordon*
A NIDA graduate, Jim Holt's television credits include *Under Capricorn* for the South Australian Film Corporation, *Return to Eden*, *Patrol Boat*, *A Country Practice*, *The Disappearance of Azaria Chamberlain* and *Bodyline*.

Dingo is a street-wise operator: con man, small-time SP, bludger. He joins up to escape the responsibility for a pregnancy and for a time fools the boys with his con-man charm. Then the facade cracks. Braggart, coward, loner and misfit, Dingo earns his nickname and shows us a contemptible side to the Australian character.

JONATHAN SWEET – *Bill 'the Pom' Harris*
Jonathan Sweet was born in India, where his Australian father worked as a marine engineer, and was educated at the English public school Charterhouse. He returned to Australia to study acting, and graduated from NIDA.

He has appeared in various German and English television programs and series, and his recent appearances on Australian television include *Special Squad*, *Carson's Law*, *Prisoner* and *Jonah*, in which he played the lead.

Bill came to Australia in 1908 and spent six years knocking around the cities and the outback, working at any job that came his way. Bill is no whingeing pommy bastard: he's a tough mate and a good soldier.

Though he does his best to hide it (and sometimes fails), he has served as a regular in the British Army. There is an air of mystery about his previous service (in India), and he wants to forget the past. We suspect that he had to leave the British Army under a cloud and in a hurry.

JON BLAKE – *Flanagan*
New Zealand-born Jon Blake has lived most of his life in Australia – long enough for him to pick up the right accent to play Slim Dusty as a youth in the film *The Slim Dusty Story*.

He played the lead in *Freedom* for the South Australian Film Corporation, and his television credits include *A Country Practice*, *Special Squad*, *Five Mile Creek*, *The Boy and the Bush*, *Patrol Boat* and *Waterloo Station*.

Flanagan (we never hear his given name) reached Gallipoli with the first group of reinforcements, just after Dick's death at Lone Pine. He and Martin become friends. But there is an inner quality in Flanagan that discourages intimacy.

Flanagan is quick to learn the soldier's craft at Anzac; in fact, he becomes a master of it in six months. Having had a rough-and-tumble upbringing, he has no romantic illusions about the war or anything else.

He follows Martin up through the ranks, always one step behind, but regards this as fortunate rather than as a cause for envy. Their relationship is based on mutual respect rather than affection, and can be stormy.

As Dick Baker represents the raw Gallipoli hero, Flanagan typifies that solid corps of highly professional fighting soldiers who emerged in the AIF in the latter half of the war.

SHANE BRIANT – *Kaiser Schmidt*
London-born Shane Briant has had an extensive career in theatre, film and television in Europe and America. Nominated for the London Critics Most Promising Newcomer award, he has played leading roles in Hammer films and in ITV, BBC, NBC and ABC productions. He was Sir Clifford in Just Jaeklin's film *Lady Chatterley's Lover* and appears in the South Australian Film Corporation production *Run Chrissie Run*.

Kaiser Schmidt is a farmer-winegrower from the Western District, at first ostracized within the platoon for his German origin. He quickly proves himself an able soldier, however, and, because of his background, is the character through whom we see and feel the Germans, so that they are not caricatures.

MEGAN WILLIAMS – *Sister Kate Baker*
Megan Williams trained at the Australian Theatre for Young People and went on to play the gamut of roles, from pantos to *Peer Gynt*. She is best known for her work in *The Sullivans*, in which she appeared regularly from 1977 to 1982.

Kate Baker enlists as a nursing sister at the outbreak of war and is given the rank of lieutenant. A working-class girl, she has brains, guts and good looks, and, when their relationship deepens, she makes a natural partner for Martin Barrington.

The question of their marrying is a vexed one. She does not believe that she could ever be acceptable as the mistress of Hereford Downs – though her spirit and beauty captivate a segment of London society. Later she comes to believe that, in any case, Martin cannot survive the war.

She is the sort of girl the newspapers back home tut-tutted about, with regard to the behaviour of Australian nurses overseas. As Flanagan is the new man of the 1920s, Kate is the emerging new woman.

NOEL TREVARTHAN – *Field Marshal Haig*
A fifth-generation New Zealander, Noel Trevarthan spent twenty-five years in London before coming to Australia in 1977. In that time he appeared in many feature films and television series, among them *The Rag Trade*, *The Avengers*, *Pathfinders*, *The New Avengers* and *Riviera Police*. He was under contract to Paramount Pictures and was an announcer and interviewer on ATV London Television. In Australia he has had numerous television roles – none better known than Gerard in *Carson's Law*.

Field Marshal Haig's rigid view of war and his attitude to the Australians may be best summed up by what he said to a group of Australian journalists in 1917, after the AIF had performed great feats: 'There is not enough discipline behind the lines, and there will not be until Australia introduces the death penalty for its soldiers!'

MARK HEMBROW – *Dick Baker*
Mark Hembrow developed a big following as the rock and roll singer Georgie Saint in *The Young Doctors*. He appeared in the film *Southern Cross* and has had a varied career in stage drama.

Dick Baker is Kate's brother and the friend since boyhood of Martin Barrington. Martin enlists 'to be with Dick'. Their brotherhood engages both of them in the high drama of war.

RHYS MCCONNOCHIE – *Lloyd George*
An actor with a prodigious list of credits in the West End, for the Royal Shakespeare Company, the BBC and Granada Television, Rhys McConnochie was most recently seen in the film of *The Wild Duck*, with Liv Ullmann, and in the television mini-series *Bodyline*.

Lloyd George, with his humble Welsh background, was able to understand Keith Murdoch and Billy Hughes on their own terms. He could not understand Haig – and their inability to come to terms is one of the high dramas of history and perhaps one of the greater tragedies of the war.

CHRISTOPHER CUMMINS – *Roly Collins*
Chris Cummins was in his final year at Sydney Acting School when he was chosen for the role of Jim Marston in the South Australian Film Corporation's *Robbery Under Arms*. In *ANZACS*, he again plays a major role.

Roly Collins is afraid the war will be over before he gets there and enlists, under-age. During the course of the war, he grows from boy to man, and in many ways we see the platoon through his eyes.

Whenever possible, he is seen recording his observations on paper. The war will affect Roly's nature more than that of any of the other characters.

Megan Williams (Kate Baker)

Mark Hembrow (Dick Baker)

Rhys McConnochie (Lloyd George)

Noel Trevarthan (Haig)

Christopher Cummins (Roly Collins)

David Bradshaw (Murdoch)

Leah Steventon (Marie) and Elaine Lee (Madame)

Peter Finlay (Bluey)

Alec Wilson (Pudden)

DAVID BRADSHAW – *Keith Murdoch*
David Bradshaw is a stage and television actor and a graduate of the Victorian College of the Arts. He has played leading roles in *Robbery Under Arms*, *Five-Mile Creek*, *A Thousand Skies* and Crawford's *Fortress*.

Keith Murdoch (father of publisher Rupert Murdoch) was a war correspondent with great political influence during the Great War. His reports to the British War Cabinet hastened the evacuation of Gallipoli. His role as 'unofficial adviser' to the Australian Prime Minister, Billy Hughes, gave him an influential voice in the affairs of the Australian forces at the Western Front.

LEAH STEVENTON – *Marie* and ELAINE LEE – *Madame*
Leah Steventon (Marie) has appeared in the ABC series *Truckies* and *Home*. Elaine Lee (Madame) has had a long acting career and is still remembered for her role in *Number 96*.

Marie admires the incorrigible Pat Cleary but brings love and sadness to the gentle Roly. Her mother, 'Madame', rules the *estaminet* and finds she has much in common with Pat.

PETER FINLAY – *Bluey*
Peter Finlay has been a writer, actor and director for the stage and also acted in John Duigan's 1977 film *Mouth to Mouth*. His television appearances include *All the Rivers Run*, *The Flying Doctors* (Crawfords), *The Keepers* (ABC), *Prisoner* (Grundys) and the mini-series *All the Rivers Run*.

Bluey is the Lewis gunner. He represents the soldiers whose deeds are remembered, but whose names and personalities have been lost in time.

ALEC WILSON – *Pudden Parsons*
A relative newcomer to acting, Alec Wilson has won an important role in *ANZACS*. He comes from a South Australian farming family, and his horsemanship helped him win a part in the South Australian Film Corporation's *Robbery Under Arms*. He has also done commercial and documentary work and had roles in ABC radio drama. He plays a prominent part in the Burrowes Dixon film *Cool Change*.

Pudden is the country boy, broad of frame, low in IQ, who shares the fortunes of the 8th Battalion throughout most of the war years.

PATRICK WARD – *Tom McArthur*
Patrick Ward cut his acting teeth at the Killara 680 Coffee Theatre and went on to the Old Tote, JCW and Nimrod. In television he played long-running roles in *Number 96*, *Class of 75*, *Chopper Squad*, *Arcade* and *Cop Shop*, and his film credits include *Stone*, *The Cars That Ate Paris* and *Chain Reaction*.

Tom McArthur, captain-coach of an Australian Rules football team, understands competition and winning. As platoon sergeant, he uses both on his climb to success. But his ruthless competitiveness hides a mass of insecurities – leading him to vacillate between heroism and cowardice.

JOHN DIXON: DIRECTOR-WRITER

As chairman of the board of Cambridge Film Productions Pty Ltd and a film and television director with twenty-five years' experience, Dixon is one of the most senior members of the Australian film industry.

The Man from Snowy River gave Dixon's career an additional dimension. He wrote the screenplay for that film, was second unit film director and is a member of the board of directors of Snowy River Productions Pty Ltd.

He brings a unique depth to *ANZACS* (which he initiated) as a Lieutenant Colonel in the Army Reserve and ex-commanding officer of the prestigious 4/19 Prince of Wales Light Horse Regiment. He was also a member of the Council of the Australian War Memorial from 1974 to 1982.

He has a prodigious knowledge of the First World War and of Australian society at that time.

GEOFF BURROWES: PRODUCER

As the initiator and principal of *The Man from Snowy River*, Burrowes has produced one of the most successful films ever made in Australia. He worked on *ANZACS* from the time he was introduced to the project by John Dixon early in 1979.

Burrowes has brought to *ANZACS* his experience in story and script development, production and, in particular, overseas sales and distribution, the latter demonstrated by his handling of *The Man from Snowy River* in the toughest of all film market places, Hollywood.

A graduate economist, Burrowes was for four years personal assistant to Hector Crawford; for one year private secretary to the Minister of the Media in the federal government; and subsequently spent three years working with Phillip Adams at Monahan Dayman Adams.

GEORGE MILLER: DIRECTOR

After fifteen years as a film and television director, George Miller is among the most experienced in the industry. That experience culminated recently in an unprecedented feat. In 1982 George directed *The Man from Snowy River*, and in 1983 he directed *All the Rivers Run*. Thus George Miller has to his credit both Australia's biggest box office movie success and Australia's highest-rating television mini-series.

George cut his teeth on hundreds of hours of Crawford television dramas including *Homicide*, *Division Four*, *Matlock Police* and *The Sullivans*. He has directed numerous other television series.

He joined Geoff Burrowes to make *The Man from Snowy River*, his first feature film. In addition to directing that film, George Miller was a principal in its development and production.

PINO AMENTA: DIRECTOR

In six years Pino Amenta has won the respect of his peers and an invitation from one of them—George Miller—to join him and John Dixon in directing *ANZACS*.

This is not the first time Miller and Amenta have collaborated. They co-directed the successful and highly praised television mini-series *All the Rivers Run*. Like much of Amenta's work, the series was a Crawford Production, and he recently finished another, the mini-series *The Flying Doctors*.

He began his directing career at Crawfords, working on such series as *The Sullivans*, *Cop Shop* and *Young Ramsay*, and for Grundys he directed *Bellamy*, *Taurus Rising* and *Secret Valley*.

Burrowes (left) and Dixon in one of Les Binns's above-ground trenches at Beveridge.

Director George Miller consults with Lighting Cameraman John Haddy during filming in the wrecked village.

Director Pino Amenta

PATSY ADAM-SMITH: STORY CONSULTANT
One of Australia's most successful authors, Patsy Adam-Smith spent six years researching Australia's participation in the First World War to produce her best-selling book *The ANZACS* in 1978.

Her research into thousands of personal accounts from the period is a perfect complement to John Dixon's efforts. Patsy was retained by Burrowes Dixon to assist in developing the characters and the plot outlines of the series.

JAMES MITCHELL: WRITER
The creator and writer of the brilliant English television series *Callan* and *When the Boat Comes In*, Jim Mitchell is regarded as one of the world's pre-eminent television writers.

He was retained by Burrowes Dixon for a year as a script consultant and to assist in writing and script editing. In this role, Mitchell spent over four months working with Burrowes and Dixon in Australia.

JOHN CLARKE: WRITER
Born in New Zealand, John Clarke came to Australia in a package named 'Fred Dagg', a character who enjoyed cult acclaim in New Zealand and Australia after being discovered on ABC radio. Later he was removed from the ABC, who seemed embarrassed by the whole thing.

His writing credits include *Lonely Hearts*, co-written with Paul Cox, and the television series *The Fast Lane*, which he co-wrote with Andrew Knight. He has renewed his association with the ABC as sketch writer and man-of-many-faces for *The Gillies Report*.

KEITH WAGSTAFF: LIGHTING CAMERAMAN
Keith has been at the forefront of Australian cinematography for the past decade. He is one of the senior members of his profession, with more than twenty years' experience. Keith is highly innovative and committed–qualities that have seen him win almost every Australian cinematography award over the years.

He was Director of Photography for *The Man from Snowy River*, his work on this picture gaining him international recognition. He also shot the major television mini-series *Eureka Stockade* and the film *Coolangatta Gold*.

LES BINNS: PRODUCTION DESIGNER-ART DIRECTOR
Les Binns's credentials as an art director are among the best in Australia, particularly on period films. Trained in the Crawford tradition of volume and cost efficiency, Les has since worked on many of Australia's big-budget period mini-series and feature films. He has forged a strong working relationship with Keith Wagstaff, working with him on both *The Man from Snowy River* and *Eureka Stockade*.

Les's appointment to the *ANZACS'* production team was regarded as one of the most critical appointments made.

BILL REGAN: PRODUCTION SUPERVISOR
General Manager and a member of the board of directors of Cambridge Film Productions Pty Ltd for the last ten years, Regan is acknowledged in the industry as one of the top production supervisors. Having successfully managed a large production company for ten years, he carries far more managerial clout than freelance production managers.

In addition to his role as General Manager of the company, Bill Regan has line-managed thousands of commercials and scores of documentaries and film enterprises throughout Australia and the rest of the world.

He is a skilled negotiator and is highly regarded in the industry for his integrity. His management of Cambridge Film Productions and that firm's growth and solidity over the period are ample testimony to his business efficiency.

DENNIS WRIGHT: ASSOCIATE PRODUCER

Dennis Wright left his own highly successful production company to join Burrowes and Dixon in producing *ANZACS*. An arts graduate, in his twelve years in the film industry he has trained at Crawfords, produced award-winning commercials and documentaries, run several production companies and dealt with large-scale film production logistics.

His background in creative management in the industry is widely recognized, and he was responsible for the day-to-day operations of *ANZACS*. His skill in the newly complicated field of production structure contributed greatly to the quality of the series.

BRUCE ROWLAND: COMPOSER

Bruce Rowland is one of Australia's most successful composers. His *Snowy River* soundtrack LP has sold more than 50 000 copies.

In 1982 he won the Australian Film Institute's Best Music Award for *The Man from Snowy River*, and he repeated the success in 1983 with *Phar Lap*.

THE CREW

Producer	GEOFF BURROWES
Directors	JOHN DIXON GEORGE MILLER PINO AMENTA
Associate Producer	DENNIS WRIGHT
Scriptwriters	JOHN DIXON JAMES MITCHELL JOHN CLARKE
Story Consultant	PATSY ADAM-SMITH
Production Supervisor	BILL REGAN
Music Composer	BRUCE ROWLAND
Director of Photography	KEITH WAGSTAFF
Lighting Cameraman	JOHN HADDY
Film Editor	PHIL REID
Production Designer	LESLIE BINNS
Wardrobe Designer	JANE HYLAND
Camera Operators	DAVID CONNELL MARK HAYWARD RON HAGEN
Camera Assistants	IAN THORBURN GREG RYAN DAVID STEVENS PETER VAN SANTEN
Clapper Loaders	SUSI STITT MANDY WALKER ROSEMARY CASS
1st Assistant Directors	BOB DONALDSON JOHN POWDITCH PHILIP HEARNSHAW
2nd Assistant Directors	STUART WOOD PAUL HEALEY
3rd Assistant Directors	LINDSAY SMITH PETER CULPAN
Continuity	JENNI TOSI CHRIS O'CONNELL
Gaffers	STEWART SORBY JACK WIGHT
Best Boys	PETER MALONEY JIM HUNT
Electricians	GREG WILSON DICK TUMMELL
Key Grips	IAN BENNALLACK STUART CROMBIE
Grips	JACK LESTER PAUL HOLFORD ARTHUR MANOUSAKAS LEIGH AMMITZBOLL
Make-up Supervisor	FIONA CAMPBELL
Make-up/Hairdressers	FELICITY SCHOEFFEL EGON DAHM DARYL PORTER WENDY FREEMAN
Sound Supervisor	TERRY RODMAN
Sound Recordists	LLOYD CARRICK JOHN SCHIEFELBEIN
Boom Operators	JOE SPINELLI STEVE JAMES
Assistant Art Directors	DAVID O'GRADY PETER KENDALL
Assistant to Production Designer	ROBERT LEO
Construction Supervisor	BRUCE MICHELL
Construction Foreman	CAMPBELL BURDON
Props Buyer	KEITH HANDSCOMBE
Stand-by Props	BARRY KENNEDY JOHN WHITFIELD MOORE BRIAN LANG
Art Department Secretary	STUART MENZIES
Props Manufacture	PETER O'BRIEN
Scenery Painter	ALAN SIMS
Props Runner	RICK LEWIS

Research	FAY JOHNSON
Wardrobe Mistress	MARGOT LINDSAY
Military Dresser	PHIL CHAMBERS
Costume Cutter	SANDRA CICHELLO
Stand-by Wardrobe	MICHELLE LEONARD JEANNIE CAMERON
Extras Wardrobe Coordinator	ANNA BAULCH
Extras Dresser	MARITA MUSSETT
Wardrobe Stock Control	JOHN WORTH
Wardrobe Maker	KATE WILSON
Machinists	ADA LAM ELIZABETH HODGES NORMA FOLLARD PALMINA SATUCCI
Wardrobe Buyer	JUDITH GOWER
Wardrobe Trainee	LIZ WAGSTAFF
Wardrobe Assistant	PAULINE LAFFAN
Wardrobe Runners	GRAEME LOADER GARY S'NG
Wardrobe Washer	MARILYN WILTSHIRE
Wardrobe Hands	KEVIN GAYNOR ROBYN ADAMS
Special Effects Supervisor	CONRAD ROTHMAN
Special Effects Assistant	BOB WENGER
Special Effects Foreman	FREDERICK CLISE
Special Effects Runner	TRACY WAINWRIGHT
Special Effects Hands	NICHOLAS ELIOPOULOS DAVID GILES JEFFREY SMART
Stunt Coordinator	BILL STACEY
Stuntmen	VICTORIAN STUNT ACTORS GROUP
Horsemaster	GERALD EGAN
Wranglers	RON KING DOC CUNNINGHAM
Armourer	MIKE WARWICK

Production Manager	ANDREW MORSE
Unit Supervisor	RAY PATTISON
Unit Manager	DOMINIC VILLELLA
Location Manager	PHIL MCCARTHY
Production Coordinator	JAN STOTT
Assistant Coordinator	JAN IRVINE
Producers' Secretary	HELEN LISTON
Production Secretary	NICOLA FOX
Unit Runners	DANNY CORCORAN DONALD KEYTE
Production Runners	LYDIA COVER ERNIE HADFIELD
Maintenance Man	RAY TAYLOR
Production Accountant	STAN SESERKO
Assistant Accountants	NATALIE HAMMOND VINCE SMITS
Computer Operator	MAREE HANMER
Set Carpenters	CLAUDE CONDOR RON MICHELL MAL PUNTON BOB JONES LES COWELL
Set Hands	ROSS VAINS JOHN RAAEN RODNEY ANDERSON MICHAEL EDWARDS MURRAY WILSON
Assistant Film Editors	PETER BURGESS ANNETTE BINGER
Music Editor	PETER PALANKAY
Sound Mixer	DAVID HARRISON
Music Assistant	MIKE GRABOWSKY
Optical Effects Painter	DAVID THOMAS
Production Publicity	SUZIE HOWIE & ASSOCIATES
Stills Photographer	GREG NOAKES
Casting Consultant	MAIZELLS & ASSOCIATES

Casual Casting	JAYNE CORNISH
Technical Advisers	LIEUTENANT COLONEL MIKE CLARK WARRANT OFFICER KEN McLEOD
Veteran Car Coordinator	ALAN LETHBORG
Army Liaison	MAJOR TONY WEBSTER
Unit Nurse	PATSY HEARNSHAW
Production Storeman	KENNETH TYZZER
Production Driver	RALPH PRICE
Bus Driver	KEVIN HUNT
Catering Manager	FRANK MANLEY
Catering Assistant	BEVERLEY STEPHENSON
Catering Hands	BETTY HIGGINS WILMA RYAN
Location Security	CYRIL THURLING
Foreign Language Coaches	GARY POPPER VIC AUSTIN
Laboratory	VICTORIAN FILM LABORATORY
Laboratory Liaison	PETER WATSON
Negative Cutter	WARWICK DRISCOLL
Sound-mixing Studio	SOUNDFIRM
Videotape Transfer Facility	AAV AUSTRALIA
Production Solicitor	FERNON & LUDESCHER

The producers wish to thank:
Film Victoria
Macfarlane Generators
Glen Cameron Trucking
Able Sheet Metal Industries
V-Line
Kubota Tractors (Australia)
Honda
Niva Motors (Australia)
Veteran Car Club
The Australian Army
The National Trust
Victoria Police
Shire of Kilmore
David Starbuck
The Australian War Memorial
Fire Fighting Equipment
Woolamai Surf Lifesaving Club
Yalumba Wines
Melbourne Production Facilities
Cambridge Films
Tolley & Gardiner

THE CAST

Role	Actor
Martin Barrington	Andrew Clarke
Kate Baker	Megan Williams
Pat Cleary	Paul Hogan
Flanagan	Jon Blake
Dick Baker	Mark Hembrow
Roly Collins	Christopher Cummins
Bill the Pom	Jonathan Sweet
McArthur	Patrick Ward
Armstrong	Tony Bonner
Pudden	Alec Wilson
Kaiser	Shane Briant
Dingo	Jim Holt
Max Earnshaw	David Lynch
Bluey	Peter Finlay
Lady Barrington	Ilona Rodgers
Sir Rupert Barrington	Vincent Ball
Reverend Lonsdale	Robert Coleby
Monash	Bill Kerr
Lloyd George	Rhys McConnochie
Murdoch	David Bradshaw
Ma Baker	Sheila Kenneally
Haig	Noel Trevarthan
Pompey Elliott	Francis Bell
Kiggell	Michael Adams
Madame	Elaine Lee
Marie	Leah Steventon
Australian Sergeant	Ian Walker
British Sergeant	Peter Ashby
Australian Officer	Robert Anson
Escort	Nick Antipas
Blimp	Harold Baigent
Blimp	Arthur Barradel-Smith
Hudson	Nick Waters
Cyril Earnshaw	Howard Bell
Australian Sergeant	Doug Bennett
Kelly	Christopher Berry

Role	Actor
60th Officer	David Bickerstaff
Punchy	Mike Bishop
Senior Journalist	Peter Black
Soldier	Bohdan
Lieutenant Arbuckle	Nigel Bradshaw
Young Recruit	Barry Branchflower
Base Sergeant	Rone Brindamour
Morrissey	Terry Brittingham
Nameless Oaf	Boris Brkic
Driver	Geoff Brooks
Carter	Peter Browne
Collette	Sarah Byrne
Imogen Mai	Tracey Callender
Royal Navy Officer	Bruce Carter
Man	Anthony Christie
Butler	James Clarke
Signaller	Tom Coltraine
Kiggell's Driver	Rob Constable
Karl Johansen	Tony Cornwill
British Corporal	Peter Crossley
French Mayor	Marcel Cugola
Tractor Driver	Max Davidson
Nurse	Julie Davison
Staff Officer	Rod Densley
Subaltern	Peter Eckersall
British Regular	
Captain	Michael Edgar
Captain Willis	Robert Essex
Birdwood	Reg Evans
Guide	Jim Ewing
Sergeant	Marcus Eyre
Jackson	Murray Fahey
Mrs Campbell	Patricia Forbes
Claudine	Kylie Foster
British Major	
Red Tabs	Earl Francis
Kovacs	David Frezzer
British Officer	Chris Gaffney
Man	Justin Gaffney

Lair	IAN GILBERT
Colonel Caldicott	BEN GLOVER
Old Digger	REG GORMAN
Sharkey	GEOFFREY GRAHAME
Matron	VIVIENNE GRAY
Mrs Collins	DIANA GREENTREE
German Sergeant	CHRIS GREGORY
Old Chorus Boy	DON GREY
Howard Doble	BOB HALSALL
Erik Johansen	KARL HANSEN
Lady Ellison	GABRIELLE HARTLEY
Sergeant Watson	PETER HARVEY-WRIGHT
British Major	ROB HEWITT
Blueys No. 1 and 2	F. J. HOLDEN
Digger in Brothel	DOUGLAS HORTON
Major Driscoll	PETER HOSKING
McGee	SIMON HUGHES
Upton	WAYNE JARRATT
Tommy	MICHAEL JOSHUA
Doctor	PAUL KARO
Harrington	VICTOR KAYE
14th Battalion Man	BRUCE KELLER
Colonel Don't Argue	BRUCE KERR
Blueys No. 2 and 3	TREVOR KILGOUR
Australian Sergeant	BRUCE KILPATRICK
Mrs McCallum	LORRAINE KINDLER
Yarborough	STEVE KUHN
French Singer	FIFI LAMOUR
British MP	JOHN LARKING
Wounded Tommy	DAVID LETCH
Jeremy	SCOTT LUCEY
Old German	KURT LUDESCHER
Bill's Niece	SARAH MACHIN
Brothel Madame	JUDITH MASSEY
Staff Officer	GERARD MATTE
Hans	ALEX MENGLET
Digger	DEAN MICHAEL
Young German	MARK MITCHELL
Batman	PETER MOON
Conductor	ROBERT MORAN
Smith	MARK MORRISSEY
Wounded Man	CHRISTOPHER MORTON
Quartermaster's Helper	GERRY MURTAGH
Walker	SEAN MYERS
Sergeant Major	KENNETH MACLEOD
Colonel	TERRY MCDERMOTT
Willie	CONNOR MCDERMOTTROE
Cav. Subbie	LACHLAN MCDONALD
Male Secretary	IAN MCFADGEN
Astley	ROBBIE MCGREGOR
Orderly	COLIN MCKAY
Sergeant Major	KEN MCLEOD
Blamey	GEOFF PARRY
Captain Young	EDMUND PEGGE
Blueys No. 2 and 4	DARRYL PELLIZZER
Mrs Earnshaw	VALMA PRATT
Publican	HARRY REID
Fifi	DANIELLE REIDY
Tommy	GEOFF REVELL
Lieutenant Friend	GLENN ROBBINS
Soapy	COLWYN ROBERTS
Nurse Purvis	MERADITH ROGERS
Australian Officer	GREG ROSS
Man	LINDSAY SADDINGTON
Lydia McCallum	MICHELLE SERGEANT
Blueys No. 2 and 2	KEIR SALTMARSH
Strawb	STEPHEN SCULLY
British Sergeant	JIM SHORE
Dusty Rhodes	IAN SHRIVES
General Wilson	JON SIDNEY
M. G. Tommy	HOWARD STANLEY
Blueys No. 2 and 2a	JEREMY STANFORD
Lieutenant Friend	ROGER STEPHEN
Murray	CHRISTOPHER STEVENSON
Sir Maurice Hankey	PETER STRATFORD
Sergeant Major	KEVIN SUMMERS
Colonel Mitchell	DAVID SWANN
French Waiter	JOSEPH SWIFCA
Williams	ANDREW THOMPSON
Boy in Trench	DREW TINGWELL
Quartermaster	TOM TRAVERS
Guardsman	NICK TRINDER
British Lieutenant	PETER TULLOCH

Role	Actor
Patroness	HELEN TRIPP
Cook	VERNON WEAVER
British MP	IAN WALKER
AIF Soldier	ROBERT WALLACE
British Subaltern	TIM WEBSTER
Staff Officer	PAUL WENTFORD
Lair	SIMON WESTAWAY
Accordionist	BRUCE WHEAT
Harrington's Aide	ROBERT WHEELER
Buffs Officer	GARETH WILDING-FORBES
Edward Kelly	JAMES WRIGHT
Shemstone	PAUL YOUNG
Whiz-bangs	PETER ROBERTS
	TERRY DEAN
	PETER WHITFORD
	BRODERICK SMITH
Pianist	DAVID ALLARDICE
Platoon Extras	MARTIN RABY
	CHRISTOPHER BERRY
	ANTHONY CLOUGH
	MICHAEL CROZIER
	DAVID HAMMOND
	LEN REDENBACH
	LLOYD TAYLOR
	MATTHEW JOHNSON
	ROBERT SMITH
	TIMOTHY BENMASAUD
	PETER SMITH
	TONY RYAN
	STEVE PARKINSON
	PETER LOHNER
	ANDREW BRIDGLAND
	NOEL MEMORY
	JOHN MOYNIHAN
	TIMOTHY STAPLETON